# Mint Sauce

## & other stories & poems

*Jan Fortune-Wood*
*(editor)*

Published by Cinnamon Press
Meirion House
Glan yr afon
Tanygrisiau
Blaenau Ffestiniog
Gwynedd LL41 3SU
www.cinnamonpress.com

The right of the contributors to be identified as the authors of this work has been asserted by them in accordance with the Copyright, Designs and Patent Act, 1988. © 2008
ISBN 978-1-905614-56-1
British Library Cataloguing in Publication Data. A CIP record for this book can be obtained from the British Library

*All rights reserved. No part of this publication may be reproduced, stored in a retrieval system, or transmitted in any form or by any means, electronic, mechanical, photocopying, recording or otherwise without either the prior written permission of the publishers. This book may not be lent, hired out, resold or otherwise disposed of by way of trade in any form of binding or cover other than that in which it is published, without the prior consent of the publishers.*

Designed and typeset in Palatino by Cinnamon Press
Cover design by Mike Fortune-Wood from original artwork:
Mint Sauce by Brett Mulcahy, supplied by agency:
dreamstime.com

Printed and bound in Great Britain by
Biddles Ltd., King's Lynn, Norfolk

# Introduction

*Mint Sauce & other stories & poems* represents the best work submitted to the fifth Cinnamon Press short story and poetry collection awards; a feast of diverse writing from distinctive voices, many of them emerging authors or talented writers exploring new genres

Jan Villarrubia's work particularly shines amongst the poets. The simple, crisp narratives that say so much between the lines are achingly good and we are delighted to be publishing the first poetry collection from this New Orleans playwright and writing teacher. *Return to Bayou Lacombe* will be published later in 2008. Other poets also stand out for their strong, individual voices, lucid language and ability to say something new. Marianne Jones's *Too Blue for Logic* and Jean Harrison's as yet unnamed poetry collection were too good to pass over and Cinnamon Press will be publishing their collections in 2009.

The short stories here are a real delight and choosing a winner was no easy task. The competition didn't have a specific theme, but there was a recurrent thread of loss in many guises running throughout the winning stories. Clare Jay's 'The Kielius Fish' was a strong contender from the start: the controlled, but visceral imagery and the oddness of the story beautifully communicate so much emotion without ever needing to spell it out. There's a dark edge in Pat Hillyer's 'The Shoe' along with a real feel for characterisation and the stream of consciousness in Catherine Chanter's 'What she did not know at the time' is completely absorbing, making the ending all the more strong. Ann McManus, Catherine

Matthews, Alice Jolly and Mark Wagstaff write with scrupulous attention to detail and complete authenticity, producing very different stories that share a real sense of humanity and poignancy; whilst Michele Wardall's take on loss brims with wry humour – a truly innovative story.

The winning story is notable for its quiet understatement and the ability to sustain a simple metaphor throughout its tightly written narrative. It's a story that hooks and completely takes the reader along. We're delighted not only to be publishing Shelagh Week's winning story 'Mint Sauce', but also to be working with her on her first novel, *To Be A Pilgrim*.

With such an interesting and compelling range of writing to choose from, working on this anthology has been a real pleasure and I hope you enjoy reading *Mint Sauce & other stories & poems* as much as I've enjoyed editing it.

*Jan Fortune-Wood*
Tŷ Meirion, March 2008

# Contents

# Mint Sauce

## & other stories & poems

Jan Villarrubia

## *from* Postcards from Katrina
(*A Lifelong Work in Progress*)


### Postcard No. 1

The levee broke.
It broke open and broke again and again and
Lake Pontchartain poured forth brine and pesticides that had dripped
from those clean, green lawns. It broke,
over and over, poured into Lake Vista, Lakeview, Village de 1'Est, the
                                                            Lower Ninth.
Flowed up Elysian Fields Avenue like something from
*One Hundred Years of Solitude* or the Bible or both.

### Postcard No. 2

Relatives of relatives give us shelter.
The grandmother's house in Denham Springs is balm,
complete with acres of green and a stream and an
old horse the color of warm toast that nuzzles and love nips our
    golden dog.
We don't feel homeless.

My own room, phone, TV. Click.
I stretch in the double bed, atop a goose-down quilt,
move my foot to a cool spot. The grandmother's house
has air conditioning. Click. New Orleans.
For miles it's only roofs. The rest is water.
Click. There's the Superdome.
There's the corpse in the wheelchair
covered with a white sheet.

## Postcard No. 3

My home remains under for three weeks.
Nights, I calm myself
imagining my clothes floating,
chairs, pots, paintings dance,
kiss like fish, change position.
Performance art, almost, always in progress.

I drift asleep playing this game.

Shrimp plants and sword fern sway under water.
The deaf cat left in the kitchen,
dog on the screened porch,
old woman with her pink, just-manicured nails.
They all sway and wave.
Her hair has come undone, undulates under water.
So graceful. So silent.

## Postcard No. 4

Houses burst, become enflamed. The natural gas
we count on in our kitchens runs amuck, entire
square blocks blaze, illuminate the night.
Please God, Goddess, Ancestors, Jesus,
take my house. Oh, lovely, clean ashes!

## Postcard No. 5

It is 2005, Denham Springs, Louisiana,
United States of America.
Soldiers in camouflage arrive.
A boy hands me an MRE and water in a can.
I have never seen water in a can.
The chicken cacciatore warms itself somehow.
There's even apple pie.
Later, we stand in a long line for food stamps.

# Postcard No. 6

New Orleans. Utterly still.
Everything is brown,
not copper or chestnut or russet or bronze,
a thick, relentless color that stripes around homes, gas stations, the
corner grocery store.
The long, oily line rings the whole city.
A thick layer of caked sediment coats the ground.
Nothing is alive.
It's like a ghost town from a western movie.
It's like Nagasaki.

The odor!
Hell must smell like this.
Windows yawn, foul and vacant.
Filthy curtains flutter through broken glass.
A sofa juts, half in/
half out of a picture window.
A child's bedroom in the street.
A home on top a truck.
Car on the roof of someone's home.
Home on a home.
One home smeared into another home.
American flag tangled in a stiff tree.

Orange hieroglyphs sprayed on doors
announce the dead,
not unlike the night of the 10th plague,
not unlike the blood of lambs.
Azreal in New Orleans:
*X 1 DB 9/12*

# On Writing a Love Poem for B

I don't know how to say
your laugh reminds me of jelly beans,
the red and pink ones,
and your voice sounds like the forest at dawn.
I can't explain your hands,
like Columbus, determined to push West
in your search for the spicy East.
You strut like a white turkey,
waiting for hens to lie at your feet.

You feed me deer you've killed,
flesh sliced clean from bone,
entrails left for crows.
Knives glint in the moonlight.
Kidney. Heart.

I dream of you. A poppy in my fingers
heats, turns to fire,
now sugar, now the whole of Western civilization.

I don't know how to tell you
I am the deer at your feet,
Looking up and backward into your eyes.
We both tremble,
waiting for the next shot.

# Return to Bayou Lacombe

My father moves the pirogue easily,
the paddle, like another limb.
His eyes are sharp here, sighting
owls in leaves I cannot see.
And his dog Beau used to dive from there,
going deep for bones.

Tendril-like, the bayou curves, becomes
thin, ferns brush the sides of the boat,
and moss hangs so low we
bow our heads to pass.

Lost, I am, in this gray green maze.
My father was here yesterday,
gliding, winding so gracefully.
He has never left this place.

# The Gulfport House

You know the kind, with the sleeping
porch and ceiling fans. So near the gulf,
salt winds kept it peeling.
Grew in the middle of four-o'clocks and wild
camellia trees, flourishing in that gray soil.

Mid afternoons, heat shimmered,
wavered over sidewalks.
We'd watch Mr. Pat pacing, measuring,
always measuring, a gravedigger in the war.
His mother called him to supper,
*Pat, come dig a grave!*

*It's blacker than a thousand nights,*
Grandma would say, then she'd kiss and cover us.
The train's moan filtered
through the screens, through
the rattle of the ceiling fan.
That train, The Hummingbird, would
plod along the narrow bridge
spanning the *Rigolets.*


And the time they found Mrs. Jewel,
in her house of wind chimes and cuckoo clocks,
dead three days. Her wild-eyed sister,
ever blushing, pink powder
smearing her white hair, kept telling callers,
*She's sleeping. My sister is sleeping.*

They all died. One, one more.
Red camellia blooms turning brown, dropping off.
And then a fire brushed away the house,
camellia trees, four-o'clocks.

## Denise Bennett

## Hyacinths

This Christmas
we shall have hyacinths,
green nibs pushing up
from black soil
brought from airing-cupboard darkness;
blue petals
the colour of the Virgin's dress
rising in scented columns
filling the room with fragrance.

The mystery of the bulb
urging us to the light.

# The Kielius Fish
## Clare Jay

Lilia didn't really like art; it demanded something from her – an
opinion, an emotion – that she wasn't willing to give. But beauty
was said to be an antidote for grief, and sometimes beauty was to
be found in art galleries, so she found herself wandering into the
Kunsthalle in Kiel on a chilly April morning. Her suede boots
tapped uncertainly down the shiny black floors as she looked for
some beauty, her pumpkin-coloured hair bundled into an untidy
ponytail. Lilia's boss, Rebecca, had given her compassionate leave;
she was hoping that Lilia would recover from her grief, which she
referred to as an affliction. This affliction was preventing Lilia
from functioning normally in her job as copy editor for a
computing magazine. Rebecca had advised her to go somewhere
she had never been before, and Lilia had decided on Germany.

One of the first exhibits that Lilia encountered in the
Kunsthalle was a black plastic chair, cut into pieces and hanging
by chains from the ceiling. There was no beauty in this. She
walked past alabaster busts from Cyprus, whose empty eye-holes
made her feel uneasy. Then she entered the painting gallery and
came to a standstill before a large mixed-media image of a fish.
Lilia had been to the aquarium on the river front the day before,
and had seen bright yellow tropical fish, almost circular in form,
which looked like butterflies as they flitted through the fronds.

This fish was a bold lemon-yellow and was swimming fatly
down to the right-hand corner of the canvas. Its eye was made
from the silver lid of a tin can. The artist had decorated eggshells
in pale greens and vivid yellows and then crushed them into the
thick welts of acrylic paint to create scales. Around the fish, he
had ground cigarette stubs into sweeps of purple within crimson.
Lilia noticed with a sudden jolt that inside the belly of the fish the
artist had pasted a black-and-white newspaper image of a foetus.
The collage was entitled *The Kielius Fish*.

Lilia knew that beauty could vanish at any moment. For this
reason, she stored up beauty in her head. If she saw, on the way to

work, a particularly green leaf splashed with water droplets which the sun was knifing into crystals, she would slow to look at the sight, taking a mental photograph. Changes in the light would make her pause as she breathed in the beauty, trying to store it somewhere within. Beauty, much like happiness, was an inconstant, she felt. It came and went. She walked as close to the painting as she dared, and stared at it unblinkingly until her eyes ran with tears.

The painting was wild and free. It used ludicrous amounts of paint. There were colours-on-colours: white within violet, ultramarine within cadmium yellow. The foetus was the only feature leached of colour; it hung sadly inside the fish in shades of grey. Lilia looked hard, and thought she could see the mouth of the foetus opening and closing very slightly.

There was confusion all around her, and a ringing in her ears, as though someone had hit her very hard on the head. Lilia put out a hand and felt smooth, hard coldness. Her cheek was pressed into this coldness, she realised, and the whole of her right side. The voices came again, with less of an echo this time, so that she opened her eyes in a painful squint. Faces were bent over her, and a warm hand was squeezing her arm.

'Können Sie aufstehen?' asked a man with a florid face and kindly blue eyes.

Lilia allowed herself to be helped first into a sitting position, and then gently onto her feet. She passed a hand across her face and was appalled to feel it come away wet with slime. She looked at it uncomprehendingly. Saliva, snot, tears? Her chest hurt, the breath was raw in her throat. There were four or five people standing around her, their faces sharply concerned. Lilia closed her eyes in shame. She remembered hearing a sobbing lament from a great distance. Hearing it, she had thought it unstoppable. What is wrong with that poor woman? she had thought, full of sympathy. And now here she was with signs of sobbing smeared across her face and hand. The people were talking to her again, but she didn't understand. She opened her hands to them in despair.

'Sorry,' she choked. 'I'm sorry.'

None of them replied – they stood respectfully, apparently

17

waiting for her to say more — so she looked through them and walked unsteadily from the gallery, past the reception, down the steps, and finally out into the clean air.

The following day, in the little house she had rented near an artificial lake a few minutes from the centre of Kiel, Lilia was bending to wrap a towel around her wet hair when she saw a flash of lemon-yellow in the toilet bowl. She peered closer and saw a little fish down there, as bright as a butterfly, with feathery fins. She caught her breath and watched its big silver eye as it flashed around in the water.

Should she flush it to the sea? She imagined it swimming down the Kiel Canal with joyous flicks of its tail. But she knew it would die on the way, be eaten by drain rats or battered in the U-bend pipe, its glowing yellow scales corroded by chemicals. She couldn't flush it away. She couldn't pee, either, knowing it was down there. How could anyone urinate onto an eye that sweet? Lilia watched the fish in concern for over a minute, and then she screwed her towel firmly onto her head and left the bathroom to use the downstairs toilet, with its cracked plastic seat that pinched her thighs cruelly if she didn't sit on it just right.

She brushed her teeth with her strong flexi-form toothbrush and flossed meticulously. When she looked in on the fish later, it was nowhere to be seen. She agonised that using the flush on the other loo might have somehow sucked the fish down the U-bend, where it was even now fighting for its life, perhaps stuck or with its spine crushed. She remembered seeing the faintest shadow of the spines of the yellow fish in the aquarium as they swam past at eye-level, bright lights all around them. Such fragility. Lilia wrung her hands and knelt beside the loo. She picked up the bristling black lavatory brush and tapped the surface of the water with it.

'Hello?' she said. 'Hello?' But the fish had gone.

That day, Lilia walked along the metallic blue length of the river, trying not to think of what might have happened to the fish. She watched two swans fighting — how vicious they could be! The water swirled and chased over their swooping white necks and hectic wings, their beaks transformed into daggers.

Rebecca, her boss, had used the word 'miscarriage' during her monologue about compassionate leave, even though she knew that Lilia's baby had been born alive. She knew! And yet it meant nothing to her. Lilia turned her platinum wedding ring on her finger, turned it roughly so that the engraving on the inside scratched her skin. She hadn't seen her curly-haired Scottish husband, Samuel, for three months, and the last time they had been in contact was by email, to discuss an annulment. Samuel had been in Chicago on business when their baby was born, and had never seen him. It wasn't Samuel's fault, she supposed. She released the ring and noticed that the swans were spent; their fight seemingly forgotten. They drifted apart almost casually and rocked in the wash of a passing boat.

Lilia leaned out over the water and looked at her reflection, which broke and reformed in the waves. There were hollows around her eyes. She felt as though she were looking through layers, down into the deep throat of something. Not wanting to be swallowed up, she straightened up and walked quickly away, towards the diversion of the town.

The next morning, the fish was in the toilet bowl again. Its movements were sluggish. Its scales had a duller sheen. Lilia looked at it and it looked at her.

'You're the Kielius fish, aren't you?' she said.

She felt she would cry. It needed food, so she went out and bought a tub of tropical fish food from a pet store on the high street. When she returned, the fish was flapping weakly, its spine clearly visible now, the gleam in its eye all but gone. Lilia was about to pour the fish flakes into the water, her hand poised above the fish when she realised she must get it out of this water – full of germs and chemicals. Suddenly Lilia knew that the Kielius fish needed to be taken to the aquarium.

There were no plastic bags in the kitchen. Lilia looked around desperately, her hands fluttering at her sides. There were blue ceramic soup bowls, but she wasn't sure that she felt confident enough to walk through the streets of Kiel carrying a blue bowl with a yellow fish in it. She imagined the water slopping out with every step of the journey to the aquarium, and the fish circling nervously, gasping for breath. Still, she reasoned, there was no other way. She took one of the bowls into the bathroom and scooped the Kielius fish gently into it. The fish's sunshine yellow scales had faded to the colour of sunflower seeds, and its silver eye was clouded, but seeing her distress, it bravely flicked its tail. As Lilia carefully refilled the bowl with fresh water from the sink, the Kielius fish opened and closed its mouth. Her baby had moved his mouth like that, taking short, painful gasps of air. She sprinkled rust-coloured flakes of fish food over the surface of the water, but the fish didn't respond.

Lilia dragged on her jacket and left the house, closing the front door with her foot because her hands were full. It was a race against the inevitable now, she felt. At worst, she had about ten minutes to save the Kielius fish. At best she might have half an hour. She knew how it would go. As she walked swiftly past the Kunsthalle, holding the bowl gingerly in her hands and avoiding the gaze of passers-by, she thought about her baby. The doctors had refused to save him. If he had been a fortnight older when he was born, they would have done all they could, they assured her. But he was too small, so undeveloped that giving him life support would only condemn him to a life of severe mental and physical handicap.

Lilia's only son, Jamie, had been a living doll a few centimetres longer than a felt-tip pen, with a beating heart and soft fingernails. A miniature boy with plum-coloured skin and lungs too undeveloped to breathe air. What had he been thinking, to emerge so soon from his safe sac of amniotic fluid? Jamie had lain in the palm of Lilia's hand with his knees bent like cricket's legs and struggled to live. He had gasped; small, rough gasps which must have hurt him, but he hadn't cried. Nor had Lilia – she had blinked the tears away furiously so that her view of him would not be blurred. They had so little time together, after all. The doctors had told Lilia that premature babies under twenty-two weeks would usually only live for about ten to fifteen minutes without medical intervention. But Jamie had survived for a full thirty-two minutes, his tiny mouth opening and closing as he suffocated slowly in the air.

The steps which led down to the aquarium were uneven and Lilia had to concentrate, co-ordinating her legs without slackening her pace or spilling any more of the water. The Kielius fish was completely grey now. It lay in the bowl, barely moving. The small circle of its mouth opened and closed apathetically. Lilia ran up to the ticket booth at the aquarium and bought a ticket. The aquarium man, whose eyes were startlingly green, looked at her and the soup bowl strangely, but if he saw the Kielius fish, he didn't comment. He let her through the turnstile and she entered the dark interior of the aquarium with its brightly lit tanks. For a moment, Lilia wondered why she was going to all this trouble to save the life of a fish. After all, death comes for each of us in the end, she reasoned. The Kielius fish might have had a long life already, for all she knew, whereas her beautiful foetus-child had started dying from the moment he was born. But then she saw the yellow fish, astonishing in their beauty as they darted like butterflies around the tank that they shared with a dozen plump starfish, and she knew that she had been right to come here.

Stepping right up to the floor-to-ceiling glass of the tank, Lilia gazed at the fish. They were swimming at eye level, inches from her face, so that she felt as though she were floating. The water eddied around their swirling forms and yet there was a sense of stillness and suspense. Lilia was dazzled by the luminous yellow shapes; these fish like bolts of sunshine.

Holding the soup bowl firmly in both hands, she braced herself and swam forward into the aquarium, air bubbles streaming from her nostrils. The space was light and she was surrounded by free-floating yellow fish. The fish regarded her in a friendly way, as though she belonged. Pushing out strongly with her legs, she let the bowl fall and watched as the Kielius fish tumbled gracefully out. For a moment, he hesitated in the water, grey as a corpse. Then Lilia saw his gills working and the lemon colour returning to his scales. He shimmied his tail, turned briefly to shine on her with his silvery eye, then zipped away between the fronds; bright and perfect.

Lilia felt so light. All around her was the luminous shiver of beauty. The water cooled her head.

She took a deep breath and swam out towards the open sea.

21

# Rhys Trimble

## *goshawk*

*umberslicer*
            *razor*
*pikehaft&*
      *featherblade—*

*willow*
*shard&splinter*


*the fabric*


      *of the*

*bisecting*

            *air*
      *stops—*
*at*
      *foliage*

*looks at*

      *me—yellow*

## 5 *voir de jour welsh haiku*

moel faban  :twice-white
palepelted-child,    ageless
ugly,   tightens our fingers.

sealap  ripples
chloride of estuary,   our
abandoned corrosion  &  shoes.

concrete-rind  sea
dead metaphors  &  cliché
for breakfast :  seaside  town

columnar   commuters— —
pidgeoncock  struts  unperturbed
mated   insignificance

portentous   dog-chew
on  sheep-skullsitting
here,  down,  home.

# wen

folded bookpages closed—nightlight
in the dark—a calling  into the white
i shiver,  looking with new lenses
donning old trainers—coat  over dressing gown
dropping into the moonlight—rivenlight
ice-crystal  blood beating in the echoed gloom
lovely here:  black halved by snow
nineteenth century postcard scene
dotted dimly by orange painted on tree boughs
no roads,  only the tidal roar of engines
the white-noise buzz of electric cables muffled by ice
icy needles flaying barelegs raw
& nobody does this anymore! nobody loves like this!
& i walk along the atavistic route inside
finally turning,  stumbling against our fencepost
the cat having abandoned plaintive mewing—
greets me aloof,  with a visceral
stare of sisterhood.

# Doreen King

## In the Conservatory

Are you falling now, gently through my blue-
veined fingers like this *pot pourri*
tracing a straight line
because of the pull of the earth –

settling like spring snow ready to change state
and evaporate? With a cloudy moon
in the distance, I leave the door ajar
for the infusion of night

before reluctantly clearing away your plants.
They're dying through lack of care.
Are you cross I can't even save
the red geranium you nurtured for years?

Half an hour is all it takes
and even in the stainless steel frame
I try to polish the moon we embraced –
try to make it return.

There's just some soil left on the shelf
that won't budge
no matter how hard I try to mop it up;
so ingrained, your cycle of life.

# The Bell Line
## Mark Wagstaff

When the bell line rang, me and Widge ran out, though mum said not to. My earliest memory is seeing the bell line strung over the lane at the crossing. Thick, old-looking rope hung with school bells, though I didn't know lessons then.

Stormy nights, playing snap with Widge, bundling for the fire's warmth, we'd hear the bells' hard, sour note. Deliciously cruel as big sisters are, Widge said the bells lived, that they drank the wind, wed it. They were the night's music, that tidal sound from the lane, riding each breeze through the beets and potatoes, a warning not to go too far.

But when the bells called with a sharp, urgent clang, me and Widge ran out. Mum's angry voice trailed us, saying not, not, not. We didn't listen. The bells meant happenings in our lane, our small, untroubled world.

A country of small places. At school kids from the village, the farms, the little cottages scattered carelessly through the fields, knew winter nights cocooned from the wind, from separation. They knew those two-mile scrambles across the black earth to football. Everyone lived a walk away, every day measured in journeys. It wasn't strange to visit a place where the lights came from a generator growling out back. It wasn't strange to play in a windmill, any silence swallowed by the per-ker-clack as the sails turned. It wasn't strange to live where the lane crossed the railway.

The railway was alien – distant, in the closeness of our days. Old women, older than mum, told us there was a station at the heel of the village, down the turn from The Lamb and Flag. But it was long vanished, razed to a patch of cinders beside the single track before my first sight of the bell line. Old men, older than mum, remembered catching the train to market, to adventure, to the sea. No seaside specials when I was small, but every couple of weeks the creeping rumble of the night trains. You'd hear, miles off across the flat land, that distant hum that became a whine that became a clank of couplings, iron engine, and vast, crushing wheels. You'd hear it brake for each path, each lane, then roar and rip as it found its speed on the straights from crossing to crossing. Powerful and alone. We never believed men drove those trains.

We shouldn't have played on the railway, but we were kids, me and Widge. Kids know everything. That den: I smell it now, where blackberries crowded in autumn, where tangled bushes kept us safe from mum's watchful eyes. Daring each other: touch a stone, throw a stone, put your foot on the track, your hand. The metal: hot with sunlight, rusty in its long patience of trains. Hunt along the sleepers, crawling tracker-style. Hide in the gangers' derelict hut, where mice rustled last year's leaves. Shouldn't play on the railway. But those were our best-of days.

Then, and the bell line. Never much down our lane. Never heard the word traffic till later. The lane was Jack Gillies' tractor; Sam Ashcroft trotting Ruby; the dustmen on their monthly jaunt for whatever wouldn't rot; sometimes lorries for the quarry when the main road in the improbable distance was busy. The road that whispered on window-lit nights; that would take me away. The lorries were long, open. They caught the bells with the lipped ridge of their tippers. The bell line rang, me and Widge ran out, mum shouting NOT. The bells were mum's duty, paid with the cottage. She made our keep mending. She had to take mending at home. She couldn't leave the bells. Her duty rang and she'd shoo us back in. We never really went in. We hung off the door, dirt and wonder on our faces. The lorries stopped at the bells, and mum would watch the drivers all the way over the track, round the hedge and safe out of the lane. She had to watch they were all the way over and write how many lorries came in a book nobody read. Tractors, horses went by. But mum had to watch the big lorries right across, clear from the railway. Had to shift anything fell off the tippers, see the rails, sunk in concrete, weren't cracked. It seemed an important job, something to be proud of. Widge wasn't so sure.

'But there's no trains.'
'Is train.'
'When?'
Always last week, or three nights back. Always some time far enough past not to matter. I'd seen the trains. They woke you in

the still country. Widge pretended she was asleep, but I knew she heard them. First the sound, along the fields, then shaking: enough to make the bells mumble in their sleep. The big engine ripped the silence, accelerating; the dark cab looking empty, the pipes and vents and grilles on its flanks screaming with frustrated speed. Then a gap for the little flatbed truck, unseen beneath the hedgerow. Then the strange, not quite rectangular box, turreted in the moonlight, creamy white, with yellow and black signs I couldn't read. Then another gap. Then the brake van, trailing out of the past. The trains would growl and hum. I listened, till the sound was all gone.

'Train last week.'

'Yeah?' said Widge. 'I never heard.'

Never by day, and I never believed old Tom and old Joe when they'd cuff my neck and say, 'Your age, young 'un, we'd have excursion to the sea.'

Never knew the sea, only in books in Miss Simpson's class. Never knew where the trains came from. Widge knew.

'Power place.'

'Is that the sea?'

'Near the sea.' Widge knew everything.

'Can we go?'

'Stupid.'

But the trains went there and back to our small shower of bells.

If I've learnt one thing in life, one thing that's mattered in all these years reaching, I'd say it would be that it's better not to know. We were country children, in our sunny scrap of backwardness and closed horizons. Happy where we thought our world was: all the world we'd need. The snake in the garden wasn't the thrilling and barely-grasped warnings in Miss Simpson's Bible. It was growing up and learning childhood happiness is a fraud: a cage that, once freed from you lose your days searching the way back in. I'd give all the hope I can't have now for one sunny Sunday with Widge.

She was older, leaving Miss Beckett's class, leaving school. Mum said Widge had to go big school. It was exciting. Go on the bus that stopped at the village turn half-seven of a morning. Go with Sam Ashcroft's brother Rick. It was exciting. But mum didn't sound excited. She sounded like a rainy night when the bells would cry and jangle, and I'd hear her go out to make sure there was nothing vexed in the lane. I was a little boy, head full of football and wishes. I didn't know that extra connection, that womanness, between mum and Widge.

She hated big school, so tough and cross with the world she couldn't say how much she hated it. Lying awake – mum sent us up early, fierce of her evening's peace – I heard what I'd barely heard before in all my small years throwing stones, playing tig, marching soldier-like over the country. I heard Widge cry. She'd cried before: falling out a tree, taking a cricket ball square in the chest or the time she twisted her ankle. But this was lying in the dark, silent-as-anything crying. My big sister, who knew swear words and cracked conkers with her hands. Those tears – like mum's silences – were a separation, a difference between her and me. Something I couldn't share that lessened me. At the weekend she was sharp with me, wouldn't play tig through the orchard, sulked and scowled till mum sent her up and left me alone. I went and threw stones from the railway, anger and hurt in my young arms, enough to fire them over the hedge and deep into the next pasture. I wasn't even sure why I was angry, except the world had changed.

'Big bruise.'

Widge was already old enough to have her bath with the door locked, to jam the handle when she got changed. She never wore skirts except for school and I caught her only by accident, going upstairs for my best book and finding her jeans' leg rolled to the knee, feeling round a purple-gold shiner. We were kids, bruises our badge of honour, the signature of our adventures. The summer before, the last good summer, we'd a league of knocks and scrapes, outdoing each other with the swollen, broken skin of tumbleful holiday daring. Country children: we'd an admiration of bruises.

'Big bruise.'

'Sod off.'

Widge knew swearing. Mum never swore, hardly spoke. But Widge was older, knew older girls whose brothers and dads dug the land. I swerved clear of their giggly gangs but knew that's where she learnt swearing. She'd mutter sometimes – if she dropped a catch, if we were climbing and the branch wouldn't bend her way – she'd mutter the words and I'd love her all the more for her easy, grown-up rudeness. Call names sometimes, out the blue, when we were walking. Say: old so-and-so, he's a such-and-such, and I'd blush, excited and proud. Mum would've beat her to hear. But Widge never swore at me. Not till then. Cuff me sometimes, which didn't hurt; or tell me to scat when she played with her girls, which did, for all I loathed them. But she never used those words to me. Till then.

I should've stayed, stood my ground, been a brother to her. But I was little, and she was cross and tough. I ran back outside, down the lane to the turning, stopped, stock still on the empty crossroads, no clue why I was there. I felt something gone inside. Not like when she pinched or poked me. Not like when she cuffed me to get things done. That was proper. That was love. This was spite and hurt: her hurt, made worse by me. This was her tears and more than tears. Separation.

And Widge got beat by mum. Mum never hurt us, never so it lasted. She told us off or punished us with her disapproving quiet. Times we got beat were times we asked, forthright, for a beating. Lighting matches in the kitchen; playing knock-down ginger on Ray Stannit with his bad leg; nicking apples; the time Miss Beckett caught us playing tig on the graves in the churchyard, though none there would mind. Mum would've beat us for the railway, but the bushes were tangled, the brambles lively, and kept us safe, under her nose. Funny to think, when we lay on the track, we never wondered if the bells might ring and discover us, not once. A conspiracy, me and Widge: fearless and safe from harm.

I jumped at the sudden clamour. The bells had ways of ringing: sly when the wind crept in their domes; stern and all together when a lorry caught their purpose; faint and broken when the big trains shook them from sleep. But this was a new sound. A jagged, awkward howling. The bells screeched into life by harsh unnatural motion. I heard mum go, clattering the stairs with her boot heels. I went after, sharply aware of loneliness and the empty bed.

Widge was on the bell line. The best climber, she'd shinned the pole and was yanking the old rope sideways, tugging the bells in sour changes they'd never rung out before. Pulling so they stretched tight with their cracked handles twisting in grey, fused knots. I'd never wondered, till that moment, who tied the bells on the line.

Mum didn't yell Widge down. Mum didn't talk: she moved. She grappled up, half-climbing the pole – never knew mum could do that – grabbed Widge's leg and pulled her, the girl screaming where the wood bit her hands. Mum got her to ground and beat her hard, her strong right hand flurrying down on Widge's body while I stood, wanting more than anything to get my sister loose. She dragged Widge up and I followed, too scared to say, too excited to stay away from the horror. Mum threw Widge on the bed and went, wordless, to check the bells.

'You 'kay?'

Shaking, howling, swearing, scalding tears would've released me. Widge throwing stones, Widge cocky and bold kept me safe. But there was no sound. She lay still. A long, level silence of empty tracks in the dark.

Mum never got letters. Cards at birthdays and Christmas from the family we never knew; one letter a year, maybe, from whoever owned the cottage. But she got a letter. I saw the postman, puzzled in the lane. Mum sent me out when Widge came back. She never did that. I heard Widge, through the window: 'It's not me, it's not me,' like a kid, not like my sister. Mum beat her.

First, the sound, along the fields, then shaking. I heard the big engine through the far country, growling impatiently as crossing on crossing, lane on lane, choked its progress. I'd never wondered who first tied the bells, and never thought of all the other crossings from the village to the sea. Did each one have its keeper's house, its children, its bell line? When the trains with their single, neat container travelled across the night country was there a change of distant bells, stirring one line to the next, a faint, wistful music as the cargo made its way?

The engines hated the crossings, I was sure; hated to have their power and purpose clipped by roads that were always empty, by bells that rang maybe every third day when the night trains were

31

long gone. Even the quarry trucks didn't come as much as they used to, the stone getting rare, the old men saying the land would give no more. On a moonless night, through a curtainless window, I saw no tomorrow. I felt restlessness chewing my bones, even as they grew longer and stronger. There was a hole where summer had been; the last good summer flown.

I turned to say something to Widge, an instinct that she wasn't sleeping, knowing that she heard the grief of changes in her heart. Her bed was made, her bears and pillows tidy on the blanket. For a second I thought the dark was a lie, that it was morning and she was ready and I'd be late for school. But there was the train, and trains never came except at dead of night.

The big engine ripped the silence, pulling off from the path down below the crossing where we'd found a bright little stream in a culvert sparkling silver under the tracks on one of our brief and endless summer adventures,. I heard the engine building noise and power along its straight road as I stared at Widge's bed, at the neatly-tucked sheets folded under. I heard the bells shift and mutter the turbulent language of the cargo as my eyes traced the slightest print on the pillow where she'd lain. And the couplings rang and the searing screech of brakes as the engine faltered. And the shouting men jumping down from the cab, yelling: the wheels, the wheels.

The police, and the soldiers, and the black van.

Everyone who ever spoke to me about that night told lies. The woman in the bright red car, who said I was going away for a couple of days till mum felt better. Like holiday, she said. Sleepover. The family in the town with their sunny garden and jolly children, who said it was nice to have me. That it wasn't forever. That mum just needed some rest for a bit. I was welcome. But they were town children: all they knew was roads and parks, cars and Sunday trips. The teachers at the new school, who said I'd settle in. Mum, when we met that time in the café, with the couple who'd taken me at the next table. She told me lies with her empty eyes, with lips saying nothing. I knew, adulthood gripping my shoulder, I never wanted to see her again.

I never went back to the cottage, the village. Not, to this day, to the graveyard. Why? There's no one there.

I'm old now, distinguished. Respected. I write and I speak about what I write. People listen. So distinguished, I didn't even flinch when the doctor rang, that autumn past, to say mum was dead. I didn't visit. Why should I? You do what you want in life, or you do nothing at all. So old, I can lie to the keen young man writing my life story. Lie about all those things. We pull up from the past, reject it, or we go down.

Only at night in this flat, the city streets streaming below me do my knees ache and burn as though covered in a murder of bruises; my hands sting with nettles, with splinters from tall trees. My fingers itch to hurl a stone, far as that oak in the pasture. My head resounds to football shouts, muttered oaths, to running; to laughter. To the only voice that ever told the truth. To bells, in the skies of yesterday, and you and me, daring the line.

# Jean Harrison

## Blank

If I had a blank canvas in front of me
it would be so familiar:

> *fogged windows in Kent, Gloucestershire, Birmingham,*
> headlamps on a motorway miles off;

> a face at the head of a table, air between us
> like the torn sleeve of a school blouse;

> side of my mother's fridge
> where I still see blurred polar bears;

> starched napkins,
> wine-glasses like shadow policemen;

> thin hair, a confused voice asking questions
> it's too late to answer;

white enamel colander
I'd like to fill with water;

chalk cliff I might dare sketch now
with all its cracks and ledges.

# Exmouth

One bar released from a bar-code –
small black upright way out on the sands
that moves a few feet to the left, stops.

I rest my hands on the matt blue-green paint
of a cast-iron railing on top of the sea-wall,
send my mind out to a figure

that has to be a woman, newly retired,
expanding forward into the haze
where grey-green water mixes with cloud

feeling light touch her from all sides
no longer crushed by bodies
processed by escalator.

The sky bends over her,
she's not aware of anyone watching,
only of flowing into the wind.

Logic says the filtering sun pays
both of us the same quiet attention,
        she's stolen nothing.

# The day I saw a rabbit

I was papering with speedwell and bugloss,
imitating the ups and downs of a bank,
smoothing petals, running fingers along veins,
pressing two blues down onto size,
brushing clear varnish over.

I sang softly
with my back to the weight
of emptiness behind me,

my feet sank into the pile of a green carpet
patterned with leaves that lay on grass
deep enough to brush my ankles
or floated on water rising against my knees.

I must have needed the wall behind me
because I saw your shoes
polished, watery, higher than mine –
perhaps you'd found a stone to stand on, your feet
a little apart with brown waves sweeping round them.
I think you'd just said something.

I was beginning to feel a tiny, shuddering kind of cold
When I looked out of the window and saw this rabbit.

# The house on Frog Island

She sees a roof above the hawthorns,
no water across or under the track,
reeds slide past the car, there's a yard
where father swings his black bag,
knocks on a white door, disappears.
what happens inside *Nothing to do with you.*

He's left her free
to stare at a wooden house,
left over from a different kind of life,
one window, covered by a blue and white curtain,
cast-iron down-pipe, row of seedy wallflowers,
black branches over a river,

the place so cut off
even the mill chimney can't spy in
to the shrunk flesh of ridged black planks
that keep him inside, upstairs in a sick room
not looking out     *I want you*
*exactly here when I come back.*

She watches two Rhodes pecking the dust,
examines a peeling green water-butt,
thinks she needn't bother with frog princes
in a place that's only called an island,
draws a face on the dashboard, wonders
if she dare get out and feel the planks.

# The Good Daughter's Guide to India
## Michele Wardall

'I'm not really understanding why you want to take your mother to India,' the Assistant High Commissioner had smiled encouragingly.

'Well, because it's a wonderful country, full of fantastic scenery, with beautiful, friendly people. Because of the diverse culture, the exciting cuisine, the spirituality and the...'

'Yes, I know this is all true. But why do you want to take your mother?'

He didn't really get it, although he was very kind and had tried so hard to understand. In the end, he had brought in the Indian High Commissioner himself.

'Where is your mother now?' he asked.

'At home, under the stairs.'

'Bring her here,' he commanded.

Ellen was prepared for the bureaucracy and red-tape in government departments the world over. She wasn't at all prepared for the High Commissioner to have tears in his eyes when she took her mother into his office. When she opened the cardboard box and removed the casket which contained her mother's ashes, the poor man wept openly. A Hindu by religion, cremation was normal to him; but keeping the end product in a plastic casket under the stairs wasn't.

'Of course you want to take your mother to our sacred Ganges to scatter her onto the holy water, so that she may continue her eternal journey' he said, sobbing. Ellen hadn't actually thought of that. Her sisters had argued strongly against their mother being taken on this so-called 'epic adventure', when Ellen had dreamed up the brilliant idea in the first place; she guessed they would be horrified at the mere mention of throwing her into what might be considered one of the most polluted bodies of water on the planet.

*

The High Commissioner had, with regret, asked to see the contents of the casket; he would have been remiss in his duty if he had not ensured the couple wasn't planning to smuggle drugs or some other contraband. Luckily, he recognized the product of a cremation when he saw it and, amidst another flurry of tears, stamped the Importation sheet.

So Ellen had succeeded in getting her mum to India, along with her fiancé David and, along with her fiancé David, had now managed to lose her. They had spent three glorious weeks travelling by bus and train, soaking up experiences like sponges, always with Mum in tow. When they rode on horseback up the Himalayan mountainside, trying to lean inwards away from the steep drop, Mum was bouncing along in the pannier. When their boat pulled through Bombay's heaving harbour to disembark at the welcoming 'Gateway of India', Mum was at the prow. And when they were sitting amidst the vast, reverent throng, all silently watching the fairytale Taj Mahal slide gloriously down a rainbow of colours under the setting Rajasthani sun, Mum had been there. Often she was tucked away in David's backpack, but, if space allowed (which it so rarely did in the overcrowded public transport systems) they had given Mum a seat to herself.

'Why don't we draw a little face on the casket, so that it looks more like your mum and less like Tupperware?' David had blithely suggested.

'David, for goodness' sake. Have some respect for the dead!' Ellen had chided.

She actually didn't think it was such a bad idea. She had already noticed a small flaw in the beige plastic which she tended to treat as the front, and she always tried to turn that point surreptitiously in the direction of the best views or points of interest. Besides, her mum had always had a good sense of humour. Ellen wasn't sure if Mum's sense of humour would stretch to being lost; and she knew her sisters' wouldn't. Of all the disasters her sisters had anticipated on this heroic journey (wars, earthquake, pestilence) losing their mother had not been one of them.

'Didn't you think to pick her up before you got off the bus?' Ellen cried, pointlessly.

'No. I didn't consider it necessary when it was just a toilet stop,' David explained. Again.

'But you picked up your rucksack!' she retorted.

'That was because someone might have nicked our money. I didn't really expect anyone would want to nick your mum in the middle of the night,' he replied reasonably. 'If you were so bothered, why didn't you take her with you?'

'Because when I got off, you were still asleep, so I thought she would be safe with you. Silly me!' And she burst into tears.

Ellen knew she was being unreasonable, but was beginning to panic now. They had been travelling on a 'sleeper' bus (a complete misnomer) across Gujarat. The bunk she shared with David was high and solid, and the driver was a traditional Indian bus-driver: fast and deadly. He had driven for four hours in the dark, speeding past everything on the road with horn blaring constantly, zigzagging in and out of traffic (threatening to tip them onto the floor at every roll) and breaking from sixty to zero miles per hour in a mere second. He had deprived Ellen of any sleep whatsoever, and had just abandoned them here, presumably because they didn't get back within the allocated toilet time. And he had her mother. What would become of her? What would become of them? Ellen dissolved into a fresh bout of sobs.

'Where are you coming from?' A voice came out of the night. This was a frequent inquiry in India, and both Ellen and David responded automatically, before considering the incongruity of being asked such a familiar question in the middle of nowhere.

'England!' they chirped happily in unison, preparing for the expected, though disembodied, follow-up question:

'And how are you liking India?'

'Oh, we love it!' came the warm, enthusiastic, though equally conditioned response. It was David who was the first to remember their predicament. 'Er, where are we?'

'You are at the Interstate Bus Stand, Sir. And this is also my home,' the voice replied. This wasn't an entirely shocking statement in this country, and David started to feel the familiar pang of remorse at the plight of the disenfranchised and dispossessed inherent in this lovely, yet harsh, land. 'Would you like to have some chi?'

The offer of tea, under the circumstances, was somewhat

unexpected; but before David and Ellen could think of the correct response a headlight came on, and they were able to see their host, and his quite substantial house (which was indeed right at the Interstate Bus Stand where passengers got off to pee in the dark.) It was lit by the lamp of his rickshaw, the omnipresent three-wheeled taxi they hadn't expected to see here, miles from anywhere.

'Chi would be wonderful!' David sighed, with what sounded like relief to Ellen, as if the nightmare were altogether over.

'Er, don't we have a bus to catch, David?' Turning to the smiling face in the yellow lamplight she explained, 'We have had a terrible disaster. We were on the bus that just had the rest stop, and it's gone without us. And we left someone, I mean something, on it. A quite valuable something, in a sentimental way. We must intercept that bus but we have no way of contacting it and we don't know where it will pull over again and it's going too fast to catch – and I want my mother!' And she wrung her hands in pantomime anguish, before bursting into tears again.

'But this is not a problem!' declared their saviour, dressed in his traditional loincloth topped with a neatly pressed white shirt, and a woolly hat to protect against the cool northern night; the ensemble completed with a beatific smile that suggested miracles can come true. 'The interstate bus always takes the same rest stops. Here it waits only three minutes, and the next one will be in one hour, at Rajkot. There the driver remains for half an hour and everyone eats breakfast. If you would like me to take you in my rickshaw we can be there before they continue on to Veraval.'

Ellen ceased crying abruptly. 'Do you work in the middle of the night?' she asked the taxi driver, sceptically.

'No, I do not. This is why I can take you there now in my rickshaw, because I am not working at night,' he replied, with a certain logic.

The next hour was arduous indeed. Rickshaws are not built for comfort, and the smell of the two-stroke, adulterated with paraffin for economy, was always a cough-inducing hazard. They screamed along the unlit desert road at breakneck speed (for a rickshaw), narrowly escaping being mowed down by any vehicles that were bigger and faster, which was all of them. Normally Ellen would have been pleading with the driver to go more slowly, but all she wanted was to have her mother back in her arms.

'Are you okay, Ellen? You're very quiet.' David caught hold of her hands, clasped in her lap.

'I'll never forgive myself if anything has happened to her. I should never have brought her here. What on earth was I thinking of? My sisters are going to kill me!' she lamented.

'You brought her here because you wanted her to have an adventure,' David soothed, 'because you care about her, and you thought it would be fun. And because you're just a little bit bonkers,' he added, helpfully.

The sun was rising when they pulled into Rajkot, and the heat and humidity was already making them feel lethargic and soggy. Ellen searched around with her hand over her brow against the glare, desperately seeking the battered old bus, her heart banging in her chest.

'Bus is there,' declared their rickshaw driver calmly, pointing in the opposite direction. Ellen raced across the road, past the nonchalant bus driver smoking outside the door, and crashed up the steps to her bunk. The curtain was open and the bunk was occupied by an elderly man and woman, a boy and an indeterminate infant, sitting eating their thali breakfast, the rice and array of curries all laid out on paper in their laps. She was so tired, but she was sure this was her bunk. Confused, she started to turn away when she suddenly caught a glimpse of familiar beige plastic resting in the corner. It was partly obscured by the wrapping from one of the delicious-smelling curries, and looked as if it were one of the family, partaking of the breakfast in front of it.

'Well, make yourself at home!' Ellen blurted out, in happy relief at the sight.

Then, noticing the quizzical expressions on the faces in front of her, she hastily reassured them: 'Oh no, it's okay. I didn't mean you. I was talking to my mother!'

\*

Ellen felt mortified now, thinking of how she had mistaken the family's beige plastic water-carrier for her mother. In any other culture, she might have been considered just a little bit crazy. She cringed at the recollection of her strident demands to be given back her bunk, before being informed that not only was it not her bunk, it wasn't even her bus. Apparently it was one of many that formed a virtual convoy along this route throughout the night, as the dignified Indian matriarch had painstakingly explained.

'So, how's the trip? Have you had the squits yet?' Amanda asked hopefully over the telephone. Ellen could picture her sister standing in her cool Cotswold cottage kitchen, while she squirmed in the 'fragrant' damp interior of the street kiosk, trying to hear above the blare of the traffic, and counting the sweat droplets which dripped off her nose.

'It's great. It's so gorgeous here, Mandy. And Mum seems right at home. In fact, I was sort of wondering, what with the Ganges being the spiritual place for people's eternal journeys and all that, I was wondering whether, perhaps, she could stay here. Maybe. What do you think, Mand?'

'You've lost her, haven't you?'

# Marianne Jones

## Shadow World

On the white wall, a black horse:
you put up your thumbs to make its ears
and you can turn your hand into a rabbit,
billy-goat, goose – look!

My grandson laughs, wants to learn the trick.
He's forgotten the rattling ghost at the door
for animals in magic lamplight.

Season of skeletal trees against silver skies,
darkening early. We press our noses
against frosty glass, look up at night,
see a reversal: on a black screen, white stars.

# A Love Poem

*for Gerry*


On the way home from the hospital
the night before your operation,
I scratched my car,
smashed the wing mirror,
drove round and round the ring road,
lost.

I don't remember what I thought about.
I didn't think
as tower blocks went past my windows again.
All I recalled was your good-natured face
and the word, *brainstem.*

In the morning, the staff called you
Hannibal the Cannibal
as they fastened you into a head frame
and played you Mozart.

I waited in the comfort of a park.
Beds of begonias
tried to spell out something
in their pink and yellow script,

but I couldn't read it,
not until later,
when you sat up
and asked for soup.

# Boat

Once we were lambs on a chalk hill,
a single rose in a mystical room.
You could sail goose-winged over the water,
glide into harbour with the swans.
My blinkered mind opened to colours
freshened as if after the rain.

Now the bridge has girders of ice.
The lines of current in the water
form thin floes. Our boat, clinker-built,
flounders into a sandbank, fails.

What does it matter on a sunny morning
with strong coffee and the Sunday papers?
Every day, I look out over the sea.

# A lie

tonight
muslin air
shrouds the garden

even the flame
of orange tulip
greys

this is how our friendship
ended

not with cut knees
or the crack of marbles
on concrete

but with the suffocation
of mist

# Martin Willitts Jr

## Winter

Based on Fredrick Remington's *Herd Boy*


The world is extinguished among snow-
white canvas & frigid colors

he huddles inward as wool-white snow
(so blinding you cannot see it,
but feel it in each brush stroke)

he follows the herd even into freezing
knowing failure means everyone dies

so he leans into it, this wind lashing
like horse reins, in the deposit of the open

so blurred there are no trees,
just ghosts of starving snow-people

the wind chatters with their bones,
as the embers of his heart smother into ash

so cold his horse folds into itself fighting it,
the frigid wolves howling distant & near

the trace of the herd dissolving under fresh snow,
the herd bellowing as a calf dies frozen in tracks

its tiny bones frozen solid & starving from no milk
as the wind spares no one, no one thing will survive

the search for the herd must continue
even if it means riding beyond death, beyond wind

# Reflected Shade & Hint of Light

Based on Claude Monet's *Water Lilies*

We need to work quickly
before light changes

it is fickle
& dashes about
nakedly
in a drifting manner

nothing is this frantic

not the grievous loss of hair
or woodpecker throttling an elm

drifting light must be seized
or it is lost
& it will never be the same

gold & purple dimness
or luminescence of faint flowers
teasing the paint

I identify with this

the water lilies tell me
*paint fast*
their pistils licking the edged darkness

so my hands become light
glowing lush as greening pools

as eyelashes flinch
& ripple

# Fall

*Linking haiku by Martin Willitts Jr. & Terrie Leigh Relf*

*— to Willow*

willow dances on light
there is grace in red flowers
a wren calls for tea

      hummingbird hovers then dips
      a fragrant breeze toward evening

frog demands: repeat!
a field of red Buddhist hats
push the sun backwards

      a cup of green tea steeping
      so many poems to read

willow is frantic:
wrens the color of frog wind
uproot poems and nap

      slumbering through the afternoon
      the sound of birds chirping

her voice climbs the walls
her knee crimson with gong cries
place tea for swelling

      pooling on the front porch
      moonlight and her tears.

# Tears

*Based on a picture by Florin Mihai*

outside
shuttering branches
are brittle bones

a concave mirror
distorts my face
into the beginning
and end of all things

broken sticks float in air.

I could insulate them;
but they would remain
attacking my window lattice,
an unwelcome stranger
rapping to get my attention.

I should store these feelings
in temporary storage
and toss the key away.

So many broken limbs,
so many broken promises.

So many hollow reeds
to make into wind chimes.

Cranes lift their sudden heads
take off into harsh winds
leaving damp grass their absence

it is the presence of absence

# Mint Sauce
## Shelagh Weeks

Imagine a Sunday, rain clattering off the broken drainpipe, the kitchen gloomy, and outside the trees bent and weeping. I am basting the lamb, pressing cloves of garlic close to the bone, tucking rosemary neatly into the fatty flesh. I turn to my children, for they have finally asked about the granny they never knew, the aunt who went mad. This, or something like this, is the story I could tell:

It is summer, always summer – except once when winter impresses itself, with high banks of snow and a park lake frozen, so I can see in its glassy world trapped leaves and a face staring back that looks like mine. But that is the winter my mother died, and I am not young at all, and it is not fit to start the story there. I sift through for sweeter fragments, offering them to my girl called Eve, to my surly son, who digs his thumb into the rolled pastry and does not believe a word of such fairy–tales. He is like me, this child, with his flop of brown hair, his green scrutinising eyes. Even as he hears me talk of picnics and sunshine, he is listening for the shard I will not give, but which perhaps he guesses at.

I am walking alone. Walking down that muddy lane, as familiar as myself, that leads to Gran's. The path is rutted and narrow and I kick stones so they ricochet off the high wall on the right. Behind the grey sheet of concrete that rises to the blue sky, lives Amelia, a girl older than me, a girl I would like to be. She is our very own bible story, a miracle child, born to a woman almost fifty. When I hear her story told, I am struck by how she becomes more real as she billows out in flowery words. Amelia's mother – a good woman, who deserved children more than some others my Gran could mention – went to Lourdes (or so some say) and, by the time she came back, was expecting her first. My Gran has no time for religion, no time for vicars and priests who come knocking at her door to wonder why she is not at church, but is instead slapping the back of her sick husband, emptying out his clogged lungs. But she laps up superstition, often tells the story of Martha and her miracle baby, and in one telling Martha is forty and in another fifty, and sometimes there is a hint of another man – or is that in the version I now tell myself?

This miracle house, with its grey wall that runs the length of the lane and blocks Gran's sun, is grander and larger than the other Victorian houses that slope up towards it. Perhaps the nineteenth century builder took this one for himself. Once, I was summoned inside those lofty square rooms and tasted what it would be like to have money, more ease in the world. In my pink ruched dress, hair in pigtails, three years younger than the other girls, I went with my clutched present to Amelia's party. I do not know why I was chosen that time. Now when I pass along the lane, scagging my hand along the rough concrete, I glimpse behind the bite of the walls, a princess life I shall one day capture: bone china, clocks that tick, tick, a fancy piano, more bedrooms than you need.

The lane smells of mud and sometimes dog's mess. I must watch my feet, skip between islands of gravel that harbour the shit. Over to my left are the back garden walls of smaller, 1920's houses – a terrace of neat homes set at right angles to the street where Amelia lives. This is my Gran's world. In this place we are all safely defined. All working class, but some are respectable, some feckless. And everyone knows how the type of biscuit you buy, the joint of meat you can afford, tells just where you lie in the pecking order, and they know too if you're faking it, living beyond your means. When my Gran pushed Gramps to buy rather than rent (and some muttered that she'd be on the street before a year was up) she shoved him up an echelon, hassled him into an affluence he thought inappropriate and unaffordable. She basks still in the ownership of her dolls' house home with its tight, neat rooms that are clean and modern. She is haunted, as she sweeps the carpets with dustpan and brush, by a childhood of gas-light, dirt, no food and a pump in the garden for water.

Today I can smell creosote because Mr Hoskins has done his shed – again. While his wife eases her bulk from bed to arm chair, then back again, he paints and shears and nips and tucks, as if all his energy and effort might sweat some excess fat off his wife, let her squeeze out to join him in the neat back garden that butts up to Gran's. Gran has no time for Mrs Hoskins' nonsense, her illness or nerves or heart. But she does a bit of shopping for her: ham from the corner shop; ice-cream that Gran keeps on the stone grate to delay its melting; fish on a Friday.

'But with a man like that, who's to know what I would do?' That's what my Gran said to mum, eyebrows raised. But no other clues. I stayed quiet, playing with the button jar, arranging the spill of jewelled colour into family groups – rich ones, circled by poor. My cheeks burned as the fire cracked and spat, but I held my breath, wanting a bigger story. What sort of man: was he weak or depraved? In my Gran's eyes most men were one or the other.

'I know what you'd do, Mum,' my own mother said. You'd put his bags out.' I wondered if his bags would be full of garden tools, of secateurs and home-made brushes and cans with wire attached as a handle.

Perhaps that's when I started to make up my stories, when hints and assertion were not quite enough – or perhaps that air, thick with the unsaid, heady and toxic, was what I always sucked upon. The stories I read in books from the library were never as scandalous as my Gran's intake of breath, the fix of her lips in tight disapproval. Like her views about Mr Hoskins. Gran had shot me a look that day as she'd got up to go and make tea. She didn't like gossip, wouldn't expect me to pass on what I heard. Mum was flicking through the paper, barely noticing I was there. I could hear the whistle screech cut short, the bubbling of water into the warmed pot. I moved the buttons into a different configuration. The cream chipped one was Mr Hoskins, the black one, as big as a penny, was his wife and then, as I moved them onto a different section of carpet, the bedroom: Mr Hoskins transformed into a muddy beige button that nudged up to the black one. That's all I did, but I felt the thrill of sex. I looked up, quick, to see if mum had noticed what awful things played out before her eyes.

Every day I go to Gran's – to take a message, to have my tea, to see if the dog has run there to scrounge more treats. And each day, as I skip down the lane I look out for Mr Hoskins. I stare at the thin man in his overalls, who gives me a mint sometimes from deep in his pocket, and I wonder if this liking for sweet things is a clue to his oddity. Today, when I peer over his hedge, the garden is empty, but the back door is open and, from somewhere inside, a woman sings. I have run down our own street ahead of mum, down our terraced road, with its fading, crumbling houses. I have dashed through Carol's alley (my sometime friend, sometime enemy from school), that alley where her black dog throws itself at the green chipped gate, barking and scrambling in a frenzy to burst out and eat me up, devour the world. Once, at a birthday party, he snapped, then sank his teeth into Mary Cole, so now he lives in the garden, in a kennel that Carol's dad made.

Today, I have remembered to look both ways before the dash across to Gran's lane. I can see the smudged yellow arrows from the game of chalk chase I played with Tim a week ago – Tim who tried to kiss me and asked to take my pants down. If I tell mum, that will be another boy she won't let me play out with, another parent she'll march round and see. By the time I get to high school in two years, I'll have a reputation – too much the princess.

A deck chair has been placed in the sun in my Grandparents' garden, and Gramps sits there, hair thin, wasting legs stretched out. The women haven't done very well with men in my family. My gramps has been ill ever since I can remember; my own dad ran off, although I have to say he died at sea, and Uncle Cyril forgets who he is and has to be brought home by the Salvation Army. Beyond the open kitchen door is Gran, a shadowy movement that makes dinner. Sunday dinner. The path, edged with flowers, grass and weeds, was once neat and trim, but now is quite hidden. A fuchsia bush, a sea of dahlias and leggy marigolds whip across my legs and tickle as I push through them. I bend to itch my leg, just where my white socks neatly turn over. I am wearing my new Clarks shoes that will last the summer, with the short, stretchy socks that slide on so soft and easy. Later in the year they'll get hard and the white will go yellow, like fading flowers.

A voice calls out to me from the kitchen,

'Fetch the mint, lovey.' Her voice wraps me in busy love, sliding me from the lazy child that had dreamed and read all day, sprawled on the bobbly settee, into Julie who stands up straight,

55

who is dependable and full of sense. Here, I become the thing she wants: the capable elder sister (as she once was). Gran has told me that when you have a sibling die (as she did, as I have) you must slew off the nonsense of games and badness; you must be good for your mother, let her continue to grieve, even when she has another baby come along to plug the gap of the one that came out wrong.

'Nice fresh leaves, mind.'

I turn back up the path, away from Gramps who sleeps, one eye half open, and plunge into wild herbs: rosemary, thyme, sage and mint. The stems scratch my bare legs, as I stand and stoop, not much taller than their straggly growth. Apple mint, pungent and green, envelops me, stirring my tongue to taste, the smell pressed deep in my mouth, in my throat. So fresh, so rich, it does not seem possible to damp it down with vinegar and water and sugar, force it back into itself to sit beside the lamb. When I carry my offering into the house, each tiny room will surely swell up and become reckless mint, a rush of greenness that expels all else. I snap at the stems and pull at the leaves, garnering a great pile, letting some drop in my haste to do this task before Susan arrives and pushes in, too. Pink Susie. Blonde Susie. Soft and sucking up Susie, who more than me, scoops up the praise and petting. So I hoover up the leaves, ripping the brown splodged ones with the green, until my hands and face are only mint, rich and green and new.

Down the path I go again, with rich meat smells billowing from inside, smells that make me impatient to sit and eat now, mash potatoes into gravy and spoon it all up. I glide past Gramps, who opens the other eye, scrutinises my life that gallops towards a future he has no chance of. His wheeze is half a greeting, half a moan, and I smile back, sad that the games of cards we used to play have been forgotten, that the space we once wriggled into – making sense together – has shrunk, even as my memory expands it.

I remember how he would talk of war, of horses and card games that eased the hunger and rain and waiting. In my child's mind, I saw it like time indoors, rain coursing down the windows, no TV, the games all stale, waiting a life-time to grow up and escape. Although I knew the real things I had to understand were the things he never told. I did not know then that those soldiers in the trenches waited for death: quick death or the more lingering kind. And now my gramps was discovering a different sort of sluggish death – that once upon a time, in the war, he might well have wished for. Only let me die an old man, he must have said, courting the devil who sometimes visits me too, and I will put up with whatever pain you like, only let me see my children and grandchildren grow. So now he is punished and dies slowly. But he hangs on hard, telling the devil he can still play a trick or two.

When I take the bunch of mint inside, Gran is stirring the gravy, the pan lids dancing and rattling, the meat inside the oven spitting. She casts me a look. Assesses. Knows instantly. A little sigh escapes, as if she guessed that I had gone dreamy again (the disease that eats me up) and couldn't be trusted to remember not to bring the old leaves.

'Put it all on the table. I'll do it later.'

'Let me do it, Gran. That's my job – the mint sauce.'

And then the latch clicks and Susie in her pink frock and snow-white socks comes skipping down, mum behind in her white gloves and the white hat that shades her evasive eyes. Gramps has struggled upright and Susie is there with a squeal, extracting his love, squeezing out the bitterness to find his sweet kernel. Everything is brightness, a light so sharp I can no longer see.

'I'll do it, Gran,' I repeat.

But she has moved to the door and is smiling, squinting out at the family group – my mother, hand resting on Gramps' arm, Susie with her arms around his legs.

Or should I stand at a distance, to grasp those other truths I have yet to make out; is this the story I should tell?

In the kitchen, as the child chops mint, and everything is spoiled by the petrol smell of creosote from next door's garden, she hears from another room, voices and song. Her mother, Rita, is plonking on the piano, humming along so Susie can sing her nursery rhymes. Once, as a child, her mother had shakily learned to play music, but because no one in that house really knew what was good, what bad, it was easy for her not to bother too much. Yet it must have seemed, for a while, as the scales marched their way up and down, that gentility danced around the house, delicately courting them all. Until Rita stopped practicing, swam in the quarry, rode her bike with the boys and was given the belt by Gramps. And by the time Julie's dad came along, fifteen years older than Rita, and liking the young ones, especially the very young ones, the piano was keeping its lid tightly closed.

Rita knows that her daughter Julie, in the kitchen, will be feeling left out, but she cannot help it that the child is strange, bound up in dreams and oddity. Sometimes Rita blames herself, thinks it is because she did not love this first one enough, always saw her as the mistake that made her have to marry. But then she consoles herself that Cyril is mad too, so perhaps such things just run in the family.

Sometimes, when Rita feels especially trapped, she lifts the walnut lid and lays her hand over the ivory keys, straining for the soft pleasures of youth that she so foolishly threw away. When she presses random notes, they play a tuneless echo of something fine she once thought she glimpsed. One day, she wants Susie – who is not her husband's child, though no one will ever know this – to learn the piano too. Meanwhile, Rita dresses like the women in magazines, like the elegant widows in black and white films. And Pied-Piper-like, she draws the eyes of a particular married man, while making her own bargains with the devil. Once or twice Rita has thought that if she could move away, bigamy might be a solution. In the kitchen, she can smell the mint sauce that makes her remember childhood, makes her recall the curly haired brother who lapped up her mother's love and then went mad.

Is this the truth, the reason my mother Rita didn't love me and ran away with a married man? Or have I stitched together a version out of the scraps Gran half told me when I lived there in my teens? I play these rough stories over and over to myself, as I sit at my grand piano, peppermint tea beside me, fingering out Mozart note by note. And each night in my dreams, in my large house (which I have called, like a ship, The Amelia) in bedrooms where children sleep and clocks tick, tick away my life – I revert to my mongrel self, straining for the past and sniffing out the lives that have fast-faded away. I drift up and down back lanes, calling out for Gran, for Gramps – even for Susie, now she is locked away inside herself. And while I bargain with the devil, asking him to let them haunt me once more, he hides away in the mint bush, whispering that I should lie, invent a truth that will conjure my mother up, mixed with white sugar and made into someone else. And in my dreams, both Gran and my mother – who is pulling off her starched white gloves – stare back, uncomprehending, because the only stories they know lie between the lines, hidden in the gaps and tucked away in decent silence.

It is still raining outside. I am chopping the mint, remembering and making up my life, even as I push on through the living of it. Evie has cupped her face in her hands and is staring dreamily out of the window, listening to my flimsy memories of Mum, Gran, their strange Aunt Susie. My son has stopped listening and is stirring vinegar and sugar together, tasting its bitter tang and screwing up his face. He is waiting for the rain to stop so he can go back into the barn and make dens or make the fires I am not supposed to know about.

'Shall I tell you a story?' Evie asks, and a flicker of malicious pleasure animates her. She turns from the garden to fix her eyes on her brother. I know she will tell of the heap of ash near the garden wall, the burnt new trousers that I have not yet decided what I should do about.

'Some stories should stay untold,' I softly say, although I am not sure if I have ever believed that.

It smells good in our house. I wonder if my children will remember that, will remember how we stirred mint sauce together while outside the rain steadily fell. Will they one day conjure me, making gooseberry tart, mixing my stories, poised between their past and future lives?

## Deborah Trayhurn

## Difficult, here on the curve

of my world, where matters slip
to keep hold of you – your life's
gravity pulls you along
the ellipse to find a curve
of your own. I imagine
in place of mountains, ancient
rocky architecture, of
fields, shopping-mall acres, you
bathed in the sun that trundled
after you, left sky without
detail, fields that look flat and
these bare mountains, while the road
by which you left tapers away

going in your direction
it flares out generously
and I see that it must be –
am preparing messages
by boomerang, please answer
in kind, from your new fulcrum

*to H*

# In lands known for wetness, full

of impediments to dry
passage, we revere bridges.
They can soar, hang, be propped
or trussed, or stayed by cables
as long as a man – hemmed in
by an inconvenient
estuary, river, or stream
and not wishing to call up
the old ferryman (who'd want
an obolus, honey-cake
for sweetening the dog that
waits on the opposite bank
if not to know his business
oh, he could do without him!) –
can escape his stranded patch;
cross stone, wood, brick, iron, steel,
aluminium, even
concrete, to keep his feet dry
his leaping desire alive.

# Even this hard rain strafing

hillsides of my umbrella
causing rivulets to run
catch a promontory arm
perimeter hem before
dropping into the cup of
a loch, I want you to see
but since a deluge ties me
to this spot, you must come, come
soon, before it is too late

after rain even this mud
tugging on the soles of boots
retaining me here, I want
to show you, so that you'll see
it does not keep me from you
deliberately, but come
come soon before it's too late

after mud even this sun
low, northern, staking my eyes
to the landscape at my back
I want you to see clearly –
that my intentions are pure:
not for the weather I stay
not for the weather you'll come
but come you must, and in time

*to S*

# Derek Sellen

## The Valley of the Temples

At the temple of Hera, I expected to find you,
where women complain of their faithless husbands,
but the heat was too great. From where you lay,
in a villa garden under a fig tree or a willow,
I must have been one of the dots on a hillside
as you watched the tourists among the columns,
crushed in the thumb and forefinger of the sun.
Perhaps you pitied them, not knowing that you pitied me.

# Paul Yoward

## Chinese Walls

Mountains ranged in thousand yard high letters
that don't scream god to me but do contain –
the hope of the rainbow – an awe more secular.

Man's strange straight tracks pass through the passes
anomalies in nature's scheme of arcs –    transgresses–
as I do, in business class, massing over

the last copy of the FT – a crash predicted
but fortunately not on this plane
overlooking the greatest aerials not taken –

my camera left festering in Beijing.
Land shrouded in solid-cloud and aspected
to light: the view of one-thousand Mt. Fujis

in my porthole – another instant – the glint
of a beacon shines: a far off galaxy,
inhabited by Mongolians in yurts

attended by me alone, as the crags
of Dow Jones excite Mr. Average
sipping a complementary beverage

that insults his liver at 60,000 ft.
Mach 2; escaping a landscape that
*pas de deux* with a grace that belies

– it is a billion tonnes of real estate.
In my head accumulates a whole
cathedral of angel-views – as snores

compete with the hum of the air con –
the privilege of this lost on the privileged;
bored by visions religions     thought you would

have to die for     but I have no hope of
                    recording digitally as images.

*- just some different perspectives a lifetime taken to make*

# Cry Baby
## Catherine Matthews

The neon light of the credit card pin machine blinked slowly, 'checking card... please wait... checking card...' Emma tried to focus on a point above the till, whilst the shop assistant, oblivious to the panic running down Emma's spine, flapped open a carrier bag and began to pack the shopping – six DVDs, two pairs of shoes, pink tracksuit trousers with a matching t-shirt emblazoned with the word 'angel', the same outfit again, this time in powder blue, and a face paint kit. Also, the whole purpose of the visit: Benji The Bear. The one item she had planned to pick up and then leave, ignoring the rows of sparkling pink plastic and the inevitable accompanying pleas. He was a replacement for Robbie the Rabbit, whose happy songs about daisy picking had been forever silenced following a run-in with the cat. Lily had been inconsolable. A trip to Toyworld and the discovery of Benji had dissolved her daughter's crumpled frown and soothed her red, dripping nose. Emma ground her teeth in annoyance at the thought of Lily's tears. Despite the bear she knew it wouldn't be long before some other horror would distract her, and the crying and clinging and hiccoughed exclamations of 'Mummy!' would start again. She glanced at her daughter, who, apart from the occasional sniff, had forgotten about the traumas of the morning and was now absorbed in stretching and flexing the limbs of her Barbie doll.

'Lily,' Emma's voice was sharp, 'stop sniffing.'

Lily sniffed and turned her face to her mother, eyes wet.

'Don't even think about it.' Emma hissed.

The shop assistant glanced up from her packing, and caught Lily's eye with a smile and a wink.

Emma gave the assistant a hard stare, 'It's called discipline.'

The assistant glared back.

'It's important to have control of your child,' Emma said.

The assistant gave a half shrug and returned to the packing, a small smile on her face. Emma felt a faint stirring of indignation.

How dare she suggest that it was fine for a daughter to just ignore her own mother? But the spit of anger left as soon as it had arrived. A kid behind a till, acne-covered and awkward, was hardly worth the effort. Emma almost felt sorry for her. She watched the assistant pack each item carefully, arranging them jigsaw-like in the base of the bag. She probably had her life sketched out: college, university, three months with a backpack, a sunny wedding day, two sets of perfect baby feet, all set out in a bold, glittering print, leaving plenty of space for the unforeseen excitements that would undoubtedly come her way. Emma opened her mouth to speak, but thought better of it. How do you explain that plans, however tightly held, are pointless; as defeating as singing in a gale – each carefully-chosen word snatched away, leaving you hoarse and unheard.

The till chuntered into life, and with a leaden lurch of the stomach Emma knew what was coming.

'It's saying card not accepted. Do you have another one?'

There was a shuffle of interest in the queue, a leaning in at the hint of a drama unfolding. Emma felt the back of her neck burn as she rifled through her bag, the pretence that she had another seemed necessary.

She smiled, 'I must have left it at home.'

'Mummy,' Lily tugged at her sleeve.

'Well, what do you want me to do with these?' The assistant pointed to the mound of bags.

'Mummyyy,' Lily's voice stretched to a whine, as she sensed that Benji might not be coming home with them. Emma ignored her and turned back to the assistant, 'I'll come back for them later.'

'How much later? We only keep things for an hour, you know.'

A tutting swept the queue. Emma could feel the stares.

'Mummyyyyy!' The tugging became more persistent. Emma snatched her arm out of her daughter's reach. Lily stepped back, startled, and sucked her breath, ready for a wail. Emma grabbed the hood of Lily's coat and yanked her towards the door, ignoring her loud, protesting squawks. Once outside and around the corner, hidden from the stares of other customers gratified by this burst of misbehaviour, Emma knelt face to face with her daughter.

'You will stop crying,' she said in a fierce whisper.

A fat tear rolled down Lily's cheek. Emma stopped herself from wiping it away; that was no way to learn.

'I have told you before. No-one likes a cry baby.'

Lily ran her tongue over her lips catching each tear in turn. She showed no sign of understanding, or even hearing, her mother's words. Typical. There was only one language her daughter understood.

'You will stop this very second or that's it, Barbie will go in the bin.' Lily squeaked in distress and clasped Barbie to her chest. 'Understood?' Emma asked.

Lily nodded and stretched her arms out for a sign that she was forgiven. Emma gave her a blank smile.

'Naughty girls don't get hugs, do they?'

Her daughter's face fell, but the tears stopped. Instead she pressed Barbie to her face and kissed the doll noisily, her eyes locked on her mother. Emma's throat tightened.

'Don't you ever put her down?' She flinched inwardly at the harshness of her own voice. Lily paused, a sudden furrow creasing her soft skin as she seemed to cast around for the right answer, then shook her head slowly. No, of course you don't, Emma thought.

Since Barbie's arrival on Lily's fourth birthday – an ill-conceived gift from one of Nick's aunts – the doll had become a fixture in family life. Emma had worried about Lily's instant love affair with this confection of blonde and pink and had tried everything to cajole her daughter back to her more educational toys. Nick had found the whole thing funny, told her not to worry, that soon enough 'Babs' would grow dull and would be consigned to the deepest recesses of the toy box. He had been right. Barbie had started to look tattered, more dishevelled than high-maintenance, and eventually spent a long winter's week outside in the garden, unnoticed. Both parents had breathed a sigh of relief. But after Nick had gone, and with no apparent explanation, Barbie had re-appeared and was never out of Lily's grasp. Emma had even been forced to buy the doll an entire new wardrobe, each ball-gown, cheerleader outfit or sequinned leotard guaranteeing a brief window of quiet. Wherever she turned, Barbie was there, her stare unblinking and – was it Emma's imagination? – with a hint of triumph in her baby blue eyes.

'Mummy?' Lily's whisper broke intos her thoughts, 'I need a wee.'

They walked home in silence punctuated by the skittering and scraping of Lily's shoes against the tarmac. The streets were empty. Huge bay windows sat draped in expensive curtains, holding vases of delicately arranged flowers; dressed, ready and waiting for the front door to slam and life to flood the house once more. Normally, Emma would glance at each window as they passed, picturing the all too familiar life inside: tasteful decoration, carefully planned bookcases, shabby but beautiful hand-me-down kitchen tables; the shine of success, a co-ordinated tight-knit of family. Today, however, Emma found herself thinking about the first trip she and Nick had made to Rome; a nervous, happy weekend of sight-seeing and hand-holding. They sat on the Spanish Steps wedged between tourists and pigeons, the sun heavy on their backs. Nick had told her he was having a great time – such a simple thing, but the happiness left her breathless. There were photos from that holiday somewhere, she was sure; somewhere in the mess of shoe boxes and dried out albums.

Emma quickened her pace. 'Come on Lily, we don't have all day.'

'Barbie's tired Mummy,' Lily said.

Emma did not reply. Lily fell quiet.

The doll had even attended the funeral. As the heavy earth clattered on his coffin, there was Barbie, swinging back and forth in Lily's tight grip – her miniature pink ball-gown a cruel flash of a different life in which, on this particular Wednesday, Emma and Lily should have been at home, Lily's chatter warming the kitchen, waiting for him to arrive back from work. Instead, they stood hunched and numb against the drizzle.

Six weeks passed, Emma remained strong – tight smiles and dry eyes. Well, she had to, her friends agreed, for Lily's sake. Besides, not wanting to put too fine a point on it, she was still young, she would heal, and on cue a replacement would be found and life would go on. If anyone had stopped long enough –

between the regretful smiles and the endless cups of tea – they would have seen that she was not strong, just disbelieving. Young men with wives and five year olds, with friends, with holidays booked and plans to watch the football, do not die. They do not simply disappear under a mess of tubes and dressings and 'we did everything we could'. They carried on. They came back with a weak smile, a squeezed hand and a joke. But even disbelief couldn't last. Eight weeks on, Emma was raw with belief. On the fourth day of belief, she spent the morning curled in a ball next to the washing machine, a teaspoon clutched in her hand.

On a long-gone wet November Saturday, Emma had stood, heavily pregnant and wilting in the fierce heat of a department store, whilst Nick agonised over two sets of cutlery. They had argued, why did he need to be so bloody fussy about these things? Because kitchenware was very important, he replied. His earnest face had made Emma laugh and they agreed to buy the second set. The curve of the teaspoon, Nick had said in a mock pompous voice, was particularly pleasing. That night, as way of apology he had suggested they watch Big Brother – her favourite and his pet hate – and she had lain on his chest, listening to the sleepy thud of his heart, cocooned in the knowledge that another tiny heart was pumping away, working hard to make two into three.

She stayed on the kitchen floor for three hours, aware but unthinking as the microwave clock winked away the time. She cried dry, wracking sobs. Lily crawled wide-eyed onto her lap and gently stroked her arms. Emma ignored her. The face was too much.

At other times a distant thud, a slamming door, would convince Emma he had come home. It had all been a mistake. She would find herself moving from room to room just in case, hoping against wrenching hope. The rooms were always empty, the noises belonging to the domestic bliss of the neighbours – putting the bins out, the slams a full stop to an argument. She would call his mobile, although it had long since been disconnected, trying to catch him out, her heart beating faster at the just-maybe of each call. On her own mobile were ten or so texts which she guarded, scrolled through, read and re-read. Inane messages about pints of milk and football practice, scattered with the occasional kiss. Three weeks after belief set in, she found Lily in the bathroom, shaking with terror. Emma's mobile bobbed in the water of the toilet bowl. Emma stared wordlessly at her daughter

'I wanted to see,' Lily whispered. 'Sorry Mummy.'

'To see what?'

'Just to see.'

Emma could get no further explanation and the texts never returned. A slap tingled, unused, in Emma's hand. She sent Lily to her room and shut her daughter's bedroom door, then retreated to her own room and sat at the end of the bed. She watched disinterestedly as afternoon turned to dusk, then to heavy evening gloom. She heard the creak of Lily's door, a held-breath pause, and then the door pulled tight again.

Three months passed. Work wondered whether she was coming back. She wasn't. Her friends, once so admiring of her strength, shrank from the spit and storm. They retreated to their companionable nights on the sofa, shuddering at the thought of how lucky they were, and how it could have been anyone, but thank God it hadn't been them.

The slam of a front door brought Emma back to the present with a start. They had reached their street. Home Sweet Home. Emma scanned the neat line of doors – number 32 probably. Janet at number 32 had been the first to close her front door whenever Emma appeared, but not the last. It wasn't that people were cruel, Emma knew that. The tenuous friendship of neighbours ran to occasional BBQs and smiles, but was not up to grief.

'I just don't know what to say.'

How many weary times had Emma heard that sentence? She did not have the words to reply. Silence filled each encounter. Emma understood that it was simpler to close the door. Now the street always seemed closed and quiet.

She tried to ignore the familiar conflict of love and dread as they reached the front gate. Her mother had suggested she sell it, considering how expensive it was and that there was barely any money coming in. Emma had not spoken to her since. Once through the front door, she darted towards the stairs, sure that the photos of Rome were under a pile of towels in the spare room.

'Look,' Lily's voice stopped Emma on the third stair.

Her daughter had collected the post and held it aloft, a proud smile spread across her face. Emma flicked through it absentmindedly as Lily stood to attention, apparently poised for her 'well done'. At the last envelope Emma's stomach dropped, she yanked open the hall sideboard and shoved it in with other letters, all branded, 'Final Notice' in angry red. She slammed the drawer shut and Lily sidled into the lounge.

Emma remained in the hall, running her hand along the dark walnut of the sideboard. The answering machine blinked lazily. It would be her mother. She pressed the delete button. Suddenly, the chirruping of children's television filled the cool quiet of the hall. Emma felt the usual pull of guilt; they had agreed when Lily was born that television was to be kept to a minimum; there were better things to fill the time. But now its nursery rhyme refrain constantly bounced around the house. It made her head ache and drowned out her thoughts. It was easier to let it play. Nick would not have approved. But then Nick had left them. Left her. You're not here anymore, she thought, so you don't get a fucking choice.

Emma drifted to the door of the lounge. Her daughter sat transfixed by the television, huddled with knees drawn up in one of Nick's old jumpers. It was stupid, Emma knew, to worry about that jumper. Its comfort had long since faded, his smell rubbed away by months of strange skin. But when Lily had claimed it for herself, Emma had taken it back, quietly removing it from her daughters' bed. She felt a hot stab of annoyance. Lily must have crept into her room and taken it back, and seemed set on mauling it; chewing the cuffs, stretching the fabric so it covered every inch of her body from nose, over knees, to feet.

'Lily, why are you wearing that please? You're spoiling it.' Emma's voice sliced through the primary coloured chatter of the TV. Lily looked up at her, bewildered.

'Don't give me that look. I have told you before, more than once. Now take it off.'

Emma stepped towards her daughter and held her hand out for the jumper. The material, which moulded to Lily's knees, had already begun to shine with wear. Lily pursed her lips and shook her head.

'Don't push me, Lily. I've had a long day. Now I will count to ten and you will take that jumper off.' She leant down and moved to yank the jumper over her daughter's head.

'No, no, no, no!' Lily shouted, arms flailing, the Barbie doll's hard plastic pushing into her mother's face.

Emma wrenched the doll from her daughter's hand, the force sending it flying across the room where it slammed into the window with a reverberating clunk. The struggle stopped. Lily dropped her arms, her body limp, and allowed the jumper to be peeled from her. In the corner of her eye Emma could see the doll – its arms skewed weirdly, eyes staring blankly at the ceiling. Her daughter crawled to the window and carefully picked the doll up, smoothed its hair, and turned back to the television. Emma dropped her gaze and concentrated on folding and re-folding the jumper, biting down on her thoughts.

'Mummy?'

'Yes?' Emma's voice came out as a whisper, the warm wool in her hands seemed to scald her skin. She needed some air.

'Can I have one of those?'

Lily pointed towards the frenetic advert which swirled around the TV screen.

'Of course you can,' Emma forced brightness into her voice, 'we'll go shopping tomorrow.'

Lily bunched her shoulders in delight and turned to share her familiar smile, but the doorway was already empty.

# Miceál Kearney

## Groundhog day

In this field of forty sheep
the trees are pallbearers.
They line by the wall;
mourn their leaves.
Their tears form a turlough,
slowly drown this field.

Dusk. Day and night effortlessly fuse.
My words are giddy. They run before me
up to the birds' nests. Eager
to greet emergent night.

But the ice on the branches makes it hard
for words to climb
onto my page. So they fall
like the leaves. Everyday,
like the trees, I stand
and watch my words
drown.


*Turlough [tur-lock]: a seasonal body of water.*

# 5 heifers

all winter housed in the yard. Fed
the freshest silage, the cleanest water.
All the nuts they could eat.

But they'd hang their heads by the gate,
longed for earth between their hooves.
Hard to run giddy on concrete,
between confining walls.

Eventually beaten with hurlies
and a black pipe
onto the back of a truck.
Destination:

| f | h | h | f | h |
|---|---|---|---|---|
| i | e | a | r | o |
| v | i | n | o | o |
| e | f | g | m | k |
|   | e |   |   | s |
|   | r |   |   |   |
|   | s |   |   |   |

75

# Shepherd

In the killing fields of my youth
the grass has been grazed skin tight.
The sheep, their white wetted fleeces
marked by the ram.
I watch night encroach.
The trees, leafless and black
against a sky heavy with rain.

The open fridge lights the dark utility,
1 need milk, am going to save the world
from my bedroom on the PlayStation.
I'll plant listening devices
in Siberian substation servers,
so the C.I.A can listen to the militias chatter.
As the milk settles,
the moon ripples in my mug.

A jar of coffee later,
last mission:
assassinate the militia leader.
Three AM– the time heifers calf.
Nearly morning. The breeze asleep.
But not the cold.

Four AM. A calf delivered,
winched into this world by the vet
as first light filters
over sleeping houses.
One last glimpse of the moon.
Cuckoo cries break the silence.
Time for bed. I'll finish
saving the world tomorrow.

# How does the sun become the moon?

When fog hangs around all day.
A veil, engulfing fields
shrouding trees and walls.
Making it hard to count sheep.

# What she did not know at the time
## Catherine Chanter

She left them. She left them careering through the dark with their skimmed headlines, half heard music, last-minute, highlighter, underliner, meeting papers and winking phones cradled in the palms of their hands. May God hold you in the palm of his hand. A blessing she remembered from a funeral, but whose funeral? The image slipped away as the doors slid open. They were the same people as yesterday and tomorrow. They left her, carrying on without her as she stepped onto the platform, the insiders who had been eyeing up her seat and the outsiders, mingling briefly, shoulder-brushingly briefly, jostling to replace her.

The station beat like a great pulsating heart, pulling some travellers down constricted veins into dark blue tunnels, and pushing others, like herself, spurting up and out in a flash of red shoes and shopping bags. Except, it seemed to her that morning, that the descending numbers were overwhelming; far more, far more than the few of them struggling up for air. She wove up the steps, between the laptopcases, whiteshirtarms and bittentothequick fingernails. They were all faceless, the comingdownpeople, and, like a lost child at a grownups' party, she was only ever level with black trousers and unfamiliar arms.

The robotic barriers rejected the passenger in front of her, but slickly sucked in and spat out her travel pass, logging her identity and her diminishing value. Then she was through, into the twilight world of station shops where the sunshine from the street formed shifting alliances with the fluorescent glow of Alan's Shoes & Keys.

Inside a silhouette: an old man holding a key up to the light.

The transformation came at the station entrance where the corner was festooned with a vast array of fruit and flowers. Something about the colours and the stall holder reminded her of the shrines in Varanasi, infused by the scent of sandalwood and jasmine. When she was young, that was, and on her travels. These thoughts – no, not thoughts but insubstantial recollections of burning pyres and airmail letters, sandals in dust and motionless fans, fluttered like moths, just out of reach of the net of her conscious mind, until one settled solemnly: the fact that it was now eight days since she had heard from Peter, in Zimbabwe. She pushed the thought down and paused instead to look at the fruit.

The woman was unable to decide whether or not to buy anything: strawberries two for a pound or here-for-the-first-time raspberries or swollen mangos or tight lipped rainbow tulips or apples, plain apples. There was something about the fractional delay which would be needed, the practicality of finding the purse and putting away the change and taking hold of the brown paper bag and talking, which all seemed too much of an interruption in her need to move forward. Half sorry. Things not done. Tomorrow, she thought, as she had yesterday, she would make sure she was prepared and put a pound in her trouser pocket.

Her new beige trousers, the combat type with pockets all the way down the leg, were probably too young for her and too casual for work, but everyone knew she had no idea. It may even be one of her lovable qualities, if she could allow herself that brave thought. Something – possibly the bananas or the daffodils – brought to mind a photo of herself aged about nine, with thick horizontal black hair and a canary-yellow polo-necked jumper, standing by a sullen pony. Caption: an early example of the protagonist's catastrophic dress sense. Her mother had knitted the jumper, a complex work of art, divided geometrically into squares and columns. Knit one pearl one. Knit one pearl one. Her stomach tightened again, this time with guilt at jumpers knitted and never worn: the purple one left behind on the straight white sheets of a bed which had not been slept in; the imitation mohair cardigan which had made her eyes red; the thick black funeral crew neck which she found suffocating, even during the frozen months of the bleakest winters.

She had been a provider, no doubt, this mother of hers. Not just the knitting, but the food. More food, have some more food, don't let it go to waste food. She still was: offering recipes and hints about sautéing on the end of the phone. We're having a lovely piece of gammon, me and your father, one hundred and sixty miles away. How are you? She should have rung last night;

would have rung if it hadn't been for… well, no excuse really, she reprimanded herself. Time goes so quickly. Definitely tonight. She'll call tonight.

The filthy bandage which encased the entire leg of the homeless man who slept at the top of the steps to the underpass was starting to unravel.

She had been able to drive to her last job in twelve self-contained minutes. Out of the door. Into the car. Out of the car. Into the door. Morning everyone. Night everyone. Out of the door. Into the car. Out of the car. Into the door. Hello. I'm home. She, like everyone else, had assumed that exchanging this for the hour long commute would be a price she had to pay for promotion. Literally pay, of course, because it was much more expensive. Cancelled out the extra money. What about the children, her mother had asked. It'll be a long day for them. Had she forgotten how old everyone was?

But what she could never have foreseen was how beautiful this journey would be. How she was no longer separated, but connected at last to the turning world. She had struggled to find a way of expressing it, but came up at last with Scottish dancing. It was almost like Scottish dancing, when you felt you had touched everyone in the spiralling room. Despite the sun, and perhaps prompted by the slamming of a car door, a memory of leaving a New Year party played at the edge of her mind: the chattering silence when the music stopped and her mother singing *Auld Lang Syne* on the way home in the front seat of the car. And they had talked about the fuss some people made, about when you were meant to link arms and how it was always either too soon or too late. And as if it mattered anyway, at the turning of the year.

The elegant couple in front of her dropped hands and kissed goodbye as they went their separate ways. She also turned off the main road, into All Saints Road where the grand Victorian houses stood legs astride and confident on either side of the quiet street where the sun never set. When she fantasised about the lottery, these houses featured on her wish list. Self contained flat at the top, with an interconnecting door, just in case Peter came back and got a job in London. Self contained room in the basement for her mother, if it came to that. She hoped it wouldn't come to that.

In this morning light, she couldn't see through their long solemn windows, but last December dark, there had been Christmas trees with white lights and small boys in pyjamas sucking thumbs, staring out at her, staring into the winter haze, waiting.

'Oh we were waiting for Father Christmas once, and guess what? We saw him! We were standing at the end of our lane.'

She loved to tell this story, this best ever, favourite memory to whoever would listen, so in her mind she had told it to the staring babies behind the glass, who, as it happened, were not waiting for Father Christmas at all.

'His musical sleigh had been and gone, out of sight, with men in anoraks shaking tins and stamping their feet in the cold, but no sign of Santa. We were all so so disappointed and I was about to take the children home, when, guess what?'

And the deaf babies were staring at the raindrops weeping on the windowpane so they did not answer.

Her voice was triumphant with remembered joy as she finished the story. 'Suddenly, suddenly, rolling through the shroud of ice and mist, there he was after all! Red and bearded and quite alone! Like a miracle! So we all believed all over again! Because there he was!'

'There he is!' A little girl was windmilling down the hill towards her. A sheepish terrier emerged from some exotic camellias, trailing his lead. 'Come back to me.' The bossy little girl claimed the dog and the mother claimed the girl. Their baby screwed sideways in the pushchair and reached out his gradually opening fist, but there was nothing there.

Seeing all the children, that was one of the best things about the walk to work: these streets were full of children going to school. Fathers now, more fathers than when hers were young: eyes looking upwards connecting with eyes looking downwards; questions and answers rising and falling with the missing the cracks and the pushing the scooter and the kicking the stones. Once, up and about unexpectedly early on a quiet October morning in Toulouse, (the light from the shutters drawing straight lines across the sweet, soft, lost curve of his naked back) she had passed French children on their way to school and felt the sad, strange familiarity of what would one day be her history.

The days when she had walked her children every day had long gone. Did her mother walk with her to school? How odd to have no memory of that. When she was older, of course, the route was a river of relationships navigated by their gang of four, treading water, holding hands in secret backwaters, ignoring the bell. One of them was Mary. Perhaps it was her funeral? May God hold you in the palm of his hand.

At the corner of All Saints and The Gardens, a child cowered in a badly parked car, sobbing. Clutching the handle. The mother yanked her arm. Get out. You've got to go. Get out. Get out. I've got to go. I can't stay here any longer.

The unexpected bluebells in the garden on the right made the city air thick and giddy. And all the

Students from Jerusalem and
Ex-pats from The Hague, and
The Pakistani businessmen and
Joggers from New York,

were momentarily embraced with her by its beechgreen springblue Englishness. The cigarette smoke from the builders leaning on the van mingled with the flowers and hung like incense over them all. She was pleased with how easily she climbed the hill, without hurrying, in her flat red walking-to-work shoes. Pleased with how she fitted in with everyone around and around, hopping on and off this morning roundabout. Only the lollipop lady was still. She stood at the centre of them all, greeting them with the sideways half smile of strangers who meet always and never and she offered them safe passage. It occurred to her that she would never know her name.

Mad and unexpected, the cavalry clattering of thirty six chargers in threes, pounding past the lone street sweeper, who paused, like her, to wonder at their naked power and the fixed faces of the twelve horsemen.

The last few yards up to the door were steeper and she slowed down. Maybe she was reluctant to arrive. Maybe there was also a reluctance to leave these living streets with their slamming doors, calling mothers and distant sirens. Her mobile rang as she rummaged for the keys amongst the jumble at the bottom of her red bag. It was inconvenient. She considered leaving it until she was inside, letting it go to message. She disliked this tendency of everyone feeling they could interrupt anyone's life at any time. But in the end, who can resist it? So she took the call as she continued searching. Listened to the disconnected voice as her fingers finally closed around her keys. Afterwards, the phone lay, inert, in the palm of her hand as she leaned heavily against the high wall, trimmed with jasmine.

Had she really come all this way without knowing that her mother had died?

# Ruth Thompson

## Apple-blossom

These days there are so many last times –
the last time he tied his shoelaces,
brushed his hair, signed his name –
small complex bonds of thought and nerve and muscle
that have gone, leaving unlit, unspoken gaps behind.

He is like a tide ebbing, at first slowly, then faster,
exposing mud flats, uneven and empty of waders.
He is leaf-frail, yet stone-touched
and mineral heavy, as though he has bathed
once too often in Lough Neagh water.

He is dwindling in transit, and snared just beyond
his atmosphere I orbit him with tender guilt,
tongue-bitten, house-bound, world-shrunk,
knowing that soon everything between us will be
as the drifts of apple-blossom we saw last spring.

# Comber Cemetery

I came here to tell him about the flocks of knot
that gathered at the lough this morning,
and how they rose and wheeled together
in their thousands, so that even with the rain
and wind I could hear the rushing of their wings.

But it seems there are other mysteries at this time of year –
this sudden bloom of graveyard grey into green and scarlet,
the sad-festive drape of holly wreaths on granite,
the tenderness of gold chrysanthemums on a baby's grave –
this strange and fleeting flowering, like a desert after rain.

# Catherine Chanter

## Fin de Saison

This is what it will be like.
An old man wiping down the skeletal sunloungers
Whilst a child slips silently through the blue pool
On the last day of October.


One elderly couple sitting
Unexpectedly cross legged on the shuffling shingle
Of the empty beach, playing cards and
Losing count in the early evening chill.

The sympathetic sun is different;
Kinder and prepared to make allowances,
Like the hands of a strong nurse who knows
You will not be here for Christmas.

# When the Iraqi women…

When the Iraqi women in the Focus Group were asked
*What one thing could be done to make a difference?*
they replied:

*I remember nudging a hedgehog*
*With my boot, into the green ditch, dead.*
Move the bodies
*I did not want my children to see the blood*
*On its armour or the smear on the road.*
From the street
*There was a grand old badger once as well;*
*Armies of flies settling on the guts spilt*
So the school children
*Onto the hot tarmac.  His head intact,*
*But crooked; his heaped body silver backed*
Do not see them
*And hunched and heavy; too raw, too warm*
*To move.  So that day, we took the long*
On the way home.
*Way home.*

# Helen Cadbury

## Vestige

*n: trace – origin Latin: footprint*

It came to her

       as she walked

              on herringbone pavia

                     looking down

                            she understood

                     that a man had knelt

          and laid each brick

       tenderly

in an interlocking V

# In the Burrows of the Nightmare

*i.m. D.P.C. 1962-2005*


There's a faceless congregation
who ask for you by name,
claim they do not know what happened,

they try to make me speak,
but my mouth is full of sleep,
I have no liturgy.

Our father, who is in heaven,
slips in and sits down
in an almost familiar room

where the furniture is oddly stacked,
jumbled against us,
he did not live to see you

pack your bags
and dance your moonlit dance,
your moonlit flit.

The room is full
of father, son and holy ghosts,
and when they ask for you again, I pray:

*Bring me the sounds of morning,*
*to milk bottle clatter me awake.*

# The Note Writer
## Ann McManus

'1/2 lb mature cheddar.'

'pt milk – semi-skimmed (green top).'

This was the stuff of my marriage. Yellow post-it notes all over the house. Sometimes I felt frightened to lift things, move a newspaper say, disturb a placemat; just in case there was another yellow post-it note stuck there, waiting to ambush me. It hadn't always been this way. At first, if I'm honest, she did it all. We were happy; in love; three children and a new house. We didn't have much money, but we were one of the first people we knew to own our own house. I was very proud of that. She did everything back then. Looked after the children, cleaned the house, shopped and cooked. She worked hard. I realise that now. At the time? No, I suppose I didn't realise just how hard she worked. I never stopped to think about it. It was just the way things were.

Then the children started getting big. She decided to take a job. The extra money was nice, but we had got used to doing without, we didn't really need it. But she wanted to 'do something else'. Funny expression, 'do something else'; there were lots of things she could have done, but her 'something else' was an office job. Oh, she loved it. She loved the order of it; imposing procedures, filing everything in its correct place. She even loved folding the letters so they were exactly one third in depth, and stamping the envelopes without smudges. Before I knew it, she was working every day. I didn't notice at first. She never did let anything at home slip, go undone. The house was still clean, the dinner still cooked, the children tidy and their homework done. Now, when I look back, I don't know when she did it all, but she did. I never noticed it not done.

I suppose it was about this time that the notes started.

'Bringing Charlotte to girl-guides. Back 5.30. Love you!'

'At dentist with Tom. See you 4.15ish. Love you!'

I didn't mind these notes. This was modern living. A way of communicating, staying in touch, knowing where she was. It was probably over a number of years that the notes began to change.

'Appt at doctors. Home 5.'
'At Church meeting. Home 3.30.'
'Simon's music recital at 3.'

At some point, the 'love you' and 'see you' got omitted. Discreetly forgotten, left off. My wife was not a forgetful person. She had instant recall of every birthday throughout the extended family. I can't believe she forgot to write 'love you', she simply stopped bothering. Perhaps she thought I had stopped noticing. I did notice though, but what was I to do about it? I mean after fifteen years of marriage you don't tackle your wife over such matters. It seemed much too trivial a thing for a man to take issue with. It would have been petty, immature, girlish. But it did aggrieve me.

Slowly the notes changed again.

'P-T meeting tonight. Pls be at school for 7.'
'Funeral at 2. Pick-up suit at cleaners.'
'Shrove Tuesday! Pls buy eggs on way home. Am working late!'

Yes, now the notes were delegating to me. Important things, justified things. Yes, I should go to my son's Parent-Teacher Meeting. Yes, I needed the suit for my Uncle's funeral, it was my suit and my uncle. And yes, if she was working late she could not be expected to shop for eggs and make pancakes when she got home and the children would be disappointed if they didn't get pancakes on Shrove Tuesday. I was always reasonable. Her requests were reasonable. It would have been churlish not to have obliged. And slowly, over time, the notes evolved.

'Pls buy ham' changed to:
'4 slices cooked ham', to:
'4 slices country cooked ham', to:
'4 slices country cooked ham – deli.'

Not only were the notes delegating, they were positively bossing and it was apparent that I could not be trusted to buy the correct cooked ham from the correct supplier. This infuriated me. In the early days, ham was just ham. She wouldn't have cared what ham was served. She would have been delighted that I had bothered to stop by and get any ham at all. I was a man on shifting sand. A few times I put my foot down and said she should buy her own ham, but my resolve never lasted for long.

The deli was just two doors down from my offices, so it was fated that I should spend my lunch hours shopping for meats and cheeses I didn't much care for. That was when I met Rachel. She worked behind the counter in the deli. At first I would read out what was on my sickly yellow post-it note, like a schoolboy sent on an errand.

'Ah, chorizo,' she said. smiling. 'I love chorizo and a nice glass of red wine.'

'Yes, gorgeous.' I hated the bloody stuff. It stuck in my dentures and was just posh black pudding. But Rachel was young, late twenties. She was to be protected from all thoughts of dentures. She probably had a boyfriend, perhaps even a husband, he would have all his teeth and the thought of a man without his had probably not yet occurred to her. Rachel made the trips to the deli bearable. I sampled Rochefort cheese, big crunchy stuffed black olives that made me want to gag, choked down slimy stuffed vine leaves and smiled as I chewed, and chewed, and chewed on a slice of Pama ham. But I never felt comfortable not trying these samples. Rachel always seemed so enthusiastic. Of course nothing ever happened. She was pretty, and about the same age as my daughter. I secretly fantasised about her. Probably every brow beaten man who entered that deli was as infatuated with the idea of her as I was. But no, she was nothing more that an imaginary flirtation. I was always the perfect gentleman. I would hand over my post-it note and she would chat whilst preparing each little carton, pressing the plastic-ridged lids in place with long thin fingers. Thankfully the paper these notes appeared on had also changed. They were no longer the tatty back of envelopes from my wife's early days of note-writing, but upgraded to yellow post-it notes, especially designed for incompetent husbands; less embarrassing to hand over to a pretty young woman than a ripped brown envelope. Sometimes hope has to be found in the smallest of places.

Every morning whilst I shaved I wondered what notes would await me that day. Probably a shopping list, perhaps a reminder, perhaps even a reminder about the reminder. There may be as many as four notes for me. Things jotted down as my wife remembered them herself. The fridge was a constant battleground. The white plastic was scarred with yellow post-it notes, pinned up like target practice. She had even been known to stick them on the inside of the front-door:

'Keys!'

I had only ever locked myself out once, but here, for evermore, or at least until the gummy lip dried out, would I have the nagging reminder.

My life had become pock-marked with notes, shopping lists, reminders. Perhaps I had grown lazy. Left my brain in the office desk. Locked it there. Secure. Redundant. Waiting to be flicked on again the next morning. Perhaps my wife needed someone to mother once the children had left. She never nagged at me, not overtly at least. It was all conducted through notes. Our whole relationship, all of our communication. I could envisage a time when we stopped speaking entirely. We could use the children's old megasketchers, save on paper:

'Good morning Dear.'

'Ah, good morning.'

'Did you sleep well?'

'Yes thanks. Can you pass the milk please?'

We had my daughter and her husband over one Sunday. She had been in a huff with her husband over some small matter.

'Oh yes Peter, she takes that after her father. We didn't speak for a whole fortnight once.'

'When was this?'

I listened intently. I wanted to know the answer as much as my daughter.

'Oh it was when your dad put his foot down over that college reunion. I wanted to go, but he didn't. A stalemate ensued for two weeks!'

'What broke the deadlock?'

'I had that scrape in the car, remember? Nothing serious, a glancing blow. But your dad rose to the occasion.'

She smiled at me then. It was a smile of genuine affection. I could have kissed her had I not been somewhat put out by the fact that to her mind we had had this major dispute and I hadn't even been privy to it. For two weeks we had apparently been in 'incommunicado', and the entire affair had passed me by. I had not been 'huffing' but here I was being accused and no-one was questioning the authenticity of the allegation. And accused in such a manner. All jokey; telling our daughter and her husband, her husband for god's sake. What else did my wife casually tell the world? If anything I was owed a 'huff'. I left the room in a rage and went and sat in the shed. Oh, I knew they'd be up there, in the living room, all cosy; laughing at my expense. 'Silly old Dad, there he goes again!' What a hoot it must be, living with me. I sat in silence until I heard footsteps on the gravel. It was my daughter. I invited her in and showed her my new DAB radio.

My wife was never much of a driver but she loved the independence it afforded her. I never had the heart to criticise her driving. She didn't even see the bus. She made a left turn and the bus ploughed straight into her. She was killed instantly. They said even a young person would have been lucky to survive such a collision. I suppose that was meant to be a comfort to me. But I felt cheated. After all these years I was sure I would go first, men generally do. And if not, then God would have the good grace to let my wife die over time. Not that I wanted her to have a long protracted suffering death. No, nothing like that. But not to die at her age in a car accident, snatched away, swatted like a flea after all the years she'd put in. She hadn't been given any time. Time was what she would have wanted. To put her things in order. Pass her jewellery over to our daughter. Decide who should have her tea-set, her mirror, her old washing board. She was fussy about that kind of thing. I knew that in her mind there would have been someone appointed for every item in the house, and every job and duty at the funeral ceremony. I searched and searched. I went through her diary, her correspondence box, her stationery drawer; but nowhere did I find a list, any list. I was at a loss. How was I to know what she wanted? And it had to be right. It must be right. It was when I was checking her belongings that my daughter came in.

'What are you doing Dad?'

'I'm looking for names. They must be here somewhere.'

'Names?'

'Yes Charlotte! Names!'

'What names, Dad?'

'The name of who should get what. I'm sure your mother will have written it on the back of this mirror. Or here, look at the base of that teapot, see whose name is on it.'

'There are no names, Dad.'

'Well I can't find one of her wretched lists, so there must be.'

My sons came in then and led me out.

To be honest, I can't remember who was at the funeral. My wife would have known exactly who was there and would have sent thank-you letters for their attendance.

In the weeks after the funeral the children called in on me every day. My daughter helped sort through all my wife's belongings. I largely took a back seat, let her get on with it. Slowly, the house was emptied of people and possessions. All the little knick-knaks I would never dust and whose purpose was unclear, went. The house became less feminine, stripped of her, de-cluttered, de-wifed. I felt that there was nothing to cling on to. Nothing tangible. For days I didn't move. Well, I went to the toilet, to bed, from room to room, but I let the cups collect in the sink, the dust gather on the television, the plants choke with thirst. My daughter called. She suggested I move in with her. Seven months pregnant and already with two children under five, it did not appeal.

'We've even got space in our garden for your shed dad. And your DAB radio.'

That was it. I had to do something drastic. I had to take action. It started slowly at first:

'Buy bread and milk.'

Lo and behold, I had some provisions!

'Buy teabags.'

Beverages!

'Buy potatoes and chops.'

I was getting good at this note thing. And before I knew it the house looked like it used to. Only more so. Yellow sticky post-it notes everywhere. On the fridge:

'Monday – chilli con carne

Tuesday – chops

Wednesday – chicken

Thursday – curry
Friday – fish and chip shop.'
On the headboard:
'Wed – change sheets.'
On the cupboard:
'Thurs – do shopping.'
On the dinning-room table:
'Sat – vacuum and polish.'
And random notes, stuck in all sorts of places:
'Do washing.'
'Ring Charlotte.'
'Iron shirts.'
'Buy birthday card for Simon.'
'Get hair cut.'
'Water plants.'
'Weed flowerbeds.'
'Shower – every day.'
'Clean path.'
'Put bins out – Wed.'
'Shave.'
'Wash car.'
'Go to bed 10.30pm.'
'Buy milk – every other day.'
'Fix landing light.'
'Set alarm for 7am.'
'Pay bills.'
'Leave house.'
'Tax car.'
'Go for walk.'
'Breathe.'
'Tidy shed.'
'Go to bank.'
'Stop crying.'
'Fix fence.'
'Paint gate.'
'Stop crying.'
'Cut hedge.'
'Miss you.'

'Clear guttering.'
'Stop crying.'
'Miss you.'
'Clean fridge.'
'Love you.'
'Love you.'
'Love you.'
'Love you.'

All the hundreds of unsaid love yous scribbled down on post-it notes covering the house. Sickly yellow, sticky, peeling, curling love yous.

# Maureen Gallagher

## No Strings

I was your whole book back then.
You devoured me.

Your window to a new world
with a word on everything,
I encouraged you
to write your
own world.

You did that
but ended up with
more characters
than space.

So you cut me down from chapter
to paragraph
to sentence
to full
stop.

Then being modern,
you dispensed with
punctuation
altogether

# Mavis Howard

## Invocation

Once upon a time, or Long long ago...
I told him our stories, sang him our songs.
He knew about thunderstorms, rainbows, dung.
He looked up to the mountains, saw the snow.
I showed him the shaman who has no shadow.
I taught him to pray to the powerful ones,
the movements to make when he heard the drums
in the night, the chant for blessing at cockcrow.
When he was small, he helped me sow corn,
walked alongside to bring in the harvest.
When the rain wouldn't come, and the rain god was deaf
to our dances and prayers, we ate the seedcorn
and he had to leave. He said he'll return
with a Kalashnikov. I say that word over
and over. Perhaps then it will rain again.

# Squeak

They didn't beat us. We were mere loose coins
picked up by chance. Maybe exchanged for ransom
or some of theirs; beheaded if nothing
came of anything. Meanwhile let alone,

food and water shoved in randomly. It could
have been the Bible, Mickey Mouse. But we had
Cleopatra. Penguin, Act two scene five.
The rest torn out. I never explained. He never asked.

At first he read haltingly, embarrassed,
couldn't get his tongue round words. I told
what went before. We sat beneath the grill,
close-sharing words and light.

I instructed him: boys playing girls, or
boys playing girls playing boys; even
boys playing girls playing boys playing girls.
It passed the time. We grew word perfect.

They listened curious at the door sometimes.
Didn't get the lingo – maybe thought it prayer. We had
each part by heart, put passion in our playing.
He played her better than any woman could.

We grew tired. He made me read all parts
but hers, sneered that I had gone
colourless, mocked my dry voice,
went silent, stood in absolute majesty.

And then I cracked. "Boy!" I screamed, and hurled
twisted words at him: "and I shall see
some squeaking Cleopatra boy her greatness –
boy her greatness". He fell on me, stuck a hand

down my throat, kicked me and the text about the room.
They rushed in, seized his hair and dragged him out.
Two months later I was blindfolded, dumped
in the desert. His body was not found.

# A Day Out in Eastbourne
## Alice Jolly

Smithy bought this VW camper van back in 1963 – dark green, split windscreen, sliding side door, 1500 cc, gas cooker, table, fridge. And room for four people to sleep – not that we slept much, Smithy and me. Shaggy hair, orange trousers, tightly fitting shirts, pretending to be younger than we really were. Sitting up high in the front and the steering wheel big as a dustbin lid and smooth to run through your hands. And the speed – scattering crows from the road, splashing through puddles, hooting at old ladies. The girls – Amber, Cindy, Joyce – were fighting to come with us – Smithy and me – on our first trip in the van, setting out from Purley down to the coast.

Oh yes, this van was the envy of all when Smithy first bought it, but now it rattles and strains, not made for this sort of road. Come to think of it – this road didn't even exist, not when Smithy and I first drove this way. I change down into second as we chug uphill. Extraordinary, really, that Smithy kept the van. Over forty years old now and worth a fair bit of money. As a collector's item, of course – not as something you'd really drive.

I look over at Smithy, sitting in the passenger's seat, fiddling around with his handkerchief. You'd think that bloody handkerchief was a wet bar of soap. He picks it up, drops it, wipes at the corner of his eye, tries to put the handkerchief back in his pocket, misses the pocket, drops the handkerchief, snatches at it, fumbles. I look away, stare out at the parched grass, the chalky landscape. Even before all this, I didn't see much of Smithy really – went our separate ways, always been quite different I suppose – but I take him out occasionally, give Joyce a break. Old times' sake and all that. But I long for the day to end. Want to get home to catch the last episode of that crime thing on the telly.

So we'll stop for a cup of tea soon? Smithy says.

I nod and smile. I'd hoped to avoid another stop but there's no way out of it now. Funny what Smithy can remember – because we have always stopped around here for a cup of tea, over the years. Somewhere between the Turnpike Roundabout and the junction where the Tin Whistle pub used to be. Joyce has packed all the necessary – table, chairs, a tin with cake and a flask. I don't know why she's sent a flask when there's a perfectly good gas burner. Does she think I'm not safe with gas for God's sake? Mind you, a flask is quicker. Get the tea over with and then only another half an hour to home.

I flick on the indicators and turn off the main road. My eyes stray to Smithy. Pick up handkerchief, drop it, search for pocket, identify pocket with other hand, try to pass handkerchief from one hand to the other, let it slip, identify pocket. Just keep your eyes on the road, Peter. The toss of a coin – could have been him, could have been you. Just thank God it wasn't you. I mean Smithy is four years older – seventy-five next birthday if I've calculated right. But all the same.

Truth is, if this was going to happen to anyone, it would happen to Smithy. He never had much luck, or never knew how to make use of the luck he had. Years and years in that teaching job, and then the buggers made him redundant. And marrying Joyce – perhaps he felt sorry for her, I don't know. A baby that only lived four weeks, homosexual son, savings wiped out in the Prudential insurance scandal. Yes, it always happens to Smithy.

He's got the handkerchief back in his pocket now, turns to me with those wandering, watery eyes, and says – A good day out. A very good day. I always like Eastbourne. Always something special about seeing the sea.

We didn't go to Eastbourne, I say. We didn't see the sea. We went to Rye. Rye's not on the coast.

As soon as I've said that, I hate myself for it. Why not just agree with him? That's what Joyce always recommends. No point in putting him straight because it only upsets him. But the problem is that now it doesn't upset him. A year ago it would have done, but now he smiles and nods quite happily. Of course, I should have taken him to Eastbourne, because that's where we always used to go, but I was tired with the driving, and didn't want to get back too late. And what does it matter anyway – he thinks he's seen the sea.

I turn down a lane – green and narrow, high hedges and grass drooping down along the sides. You don't think parts of England exist like this any more, not in the world of computers and motorways and cans in vending machines. But then you come around a corner and there you are – an open gate, an orchard, everything silent and green. I slow down, manoeuvre the van in through the gateway, get out and slide the side door open. The thought occurs to me that nowadays a field is really the right place for Smithy. In a field it isn't possible to fall down the stairs, step in front of a car, pour scalding water on yourself. The worst you can do here is put your foot in a cow pat. Perhaps that's what we should do next time, just find a field and stay there, settle down like cows.

Smithy wants to help get the chairs out, but I'd rather he didn't because God knows where that will lead. He used to have thick black hair – shaggy and hanging down over the tops of his ears – but nearly all of that has gone now, except for a few grey threads. The whites of his eyes are yellow and the skin under them sags, revealing the red inside of his lower lids. His hands are knotted red and blue. Joyce makes sure he looks smart – a collar and tie today, and shiny shoes – but somehow you can tell, just by the way he moves. The irony is that if the real Smithy were here now he'd be fascinated by this disease which is slowly eating his brain. He'd be interested in it, and amused. He'd read books about it, and know all the technical terms.

Cake, he says, and climbs into the back of the van and rummages around in there. Then he appears with a wide smile on his face and he's holding a tin in his hand, except it isn't the cake tin, it's the First Aid tin. Yes, Smithy and Joyce are the kind of people who always have a First Aid tin. But Smithy doesn't know what it is – despite the large red cross on the top – and opens it expecting to find cake. He stares at the bandages, the antiseptic cream, the scissors, the box of plasters, the bottle of milk of magnesia, and then he shrugs, trying to make it look as though the bandages and scissors have behaved unreasonably. Sliding the lid back onto the box, he guiltily edges it onto the floor of the van, shrugs, says something about how beautiful the orchard is, and shambles away.

Poor bugger – what can you do? I pull the chairs out, find the flask and get the milk out of the ice box. Smithy has left the First Aid box near the door and I fall over it as I'm lifting the table out. The same old picnic table we've always used, even when Smithy first bought the van, with money left to him by an aunt, when we were teaching in Croydon. I think back again to those trips we used to make, more than forty years ago. Stopping in some lay-by or farmers' field, drinking beers, laying mattresses out on the grass. Smithy was with Joyce, even then. Big hips, thick ankles, flat Northern accent. And I was with Cindy, or Amber, or Bella. Too many names to remember. Girls with long legs and waist-length hair and smelling of Afghan coats and incense.

I take cups out of the cupboard and look around for Smithy, but I can't see him anywhere. I climb down from the van and peer through the trees, but the leaves hang low and the ground slopes upwards so I can't see far. I start to walk, avoiding the cow pats. Smithy? Smithy? A gateway leads into another orchard and I go through it, but he isn't there. I check behind some falling down sheds. Where can he possibly be? I begin to panic.        Mustn't run, that's what the doctor told me after my heart operation, but still I hurry back towards the van. What if I've lost him? How will I explain this to Joyce? Could he have fallen into a ditch? There aren't any ditches. I head toward the gate. To the left, the lane rolls away from me with no sign of Smithy. I turn right, hurry around the corner, heading back towards the main road. And there he is, in the middle of the lane, on a blind bend, fiddling around with a tin of cigarettes and a box of matches. He must have got those out of the van when I wasn't watching.

Must have a pee, he says cheerily.

I hustle him onto the verge and snatch the cigarette and matches.

Come back into the orchard, I say, but he's intent on undoing his flies.

Must have a pee.

No, Smithy. Not here.

He's still fiddling with his trousers and I realise that if I don't let him pee here then he's probably just going to do it anyway. He doesn't seem able to get his flies undone. I push the cigarettes and matches into my pockets and try to help him. What if a car comes

105

down the lane? His zip is stuck. I tug at it, praying that he won't pee before I get it open. My fingers jerk the metal zipper but it doesn't move. I kneel down in the grass, fumbling under Smithy's shirt, until I finally manage to ease the zip down. Smithy is babbling away about something or other – butterflies, types of different grass, where this lane might or might not lead.

Come on, I say, hauling myself up. I thought you wanted a pee.

He's got hold of his shirt tails with one hand but his other hand seems to have lost all sense of purpose. I realise that I'm going to have to do this for him. I push my hand into the warm front of his trousers and take his limp prick between my fingers. I pull it out and aim. Shut my eyes, grit my teeth, pray that a car doesn't come around the corner. I make sure he doesn't pee on his shoes but drops of urine sprinkle his trousers. I do up his flies. This is the last time – absolutely the last time – I'm taking Smithy out for a day.

Could fancy a cigarette, Smithy says.

No, I say. No. And don't go wandering off. Okay? Just stay near the van. Have you got that? Just stay near the van.

I pull him back along the road and in through the gateway. I'm ashamed of my anger. Joyce does this every day and she doesn't lose her temper. I dump Smithy in a chair, and try to keep my hands steady as I pour two cups of tea. The details don't matter, I say to myself. The details don't matter. Smithy has got tea running all down his chin. The details don't matter, I tell myself again. But I can't make the bloody legs of the picnic table work. I've done it a hundred times but now it won't work. I push and pull and I feel like smashing the whole thing. Smithy rises from his chair, comes towards me, tries to take the table.

Peter. Peter, he says. Leave that table now. We don't need a table. Unsteadily he takes the table from me, lays its splayed legs on the grass and laughs, raising the palms of his hands, shaking his head at the absurdity of it all. Sit down, Peter, sit down.

That's the kind of thing Smithy always says – We don't need this, we don't need that. We have everything we need here. As I turn from the table, I stumble over the cake tin, which is lying on the ground, and knock over my cup of tea. Just like Smithy now. Old and bloody useless. Just thank God it's him not you. Except we're travelling the same road and he's only a few miles ahead. And the truth is that I haven't even got any cause for complaint because it's not as though I didn't know this was coming, not as though it doesn't happen to everyone.

Doesn't matter, Peter, Smithy says. Plenty more hot water in the flask.

Smithy is humouring me, keeping me amused, just as he's always done. A day out with Peter is always a perilous affair. Smithy knows that better than anyone. One small thing can go wrong and it'll all be ruined. So Smithy needs to keep Peter calm, damp him down, jolly him along, make sure that the day works out just right. And strangely Smithy can still do that. Turns out that kindness is what's still left, when everything else has gone. I stare at his threads of grey hair, his watering eyes, the soggy patch on the front of his shirt where he spilled his tea.

I hate him now; hate him so much that I'd like to kill him. It would be easy really – and much the best for him. There will be a jack in the back of the van. Oh yes, Smithy is a man who would always have a jack to hand. And he wouldn't even see me coming. I imagine swinging my wrist, bringing the metal smashing down onto the side of his head. I see the blood and Smithy going down into the grass. Then his eyes, still and glassy, a fly settling on his cheek, his glasses twisted and smashed, one leg spread out at an awkward angle; the butterflies still fluttering and the breeze still teasing. Hide his body away under the hedge. It would take years for anyone to find it here.

Smithy comes towards me and steers me towards a chair. My chest is heaving and I'm covered in sweat. All this isn't good for my heart. Smithy pours me a fresh cup of tea, then kneels down and slowly and meticulously tries to make the legs of the table fit together. I watch him and a word floats to the surface of my mind.

Envy. Yes, that's it. Down at the pub I always made fun of Smithy and his simple pleasures – long weekends in the camper van with Joyce, evenings sitting out in their garden, while Smithy smoked his daily cigarette and drank his one beer. Yes, I mocked him to everyone I knew, often didn't return his calls – and all the time I was jealous. Seems strange to realise that now.

Of course, I had much more talent than poor old Smithy. I didn't stay in teaching; of course I didn't – got into the marketing department at Unilever. Five bed-roomed house, holidays abroad, brand new cars. And married to Patty – long legs and waist-length hair – except she left me and the kids. And the strange thing is that I knew that she would. And I knew that the jobs and houses and cars – I knew that none of it would count for anything, finally. But still I couldn't stop myself. And now it seems to me that it was all there in the tea leaves or marked out in the stars, all those years ago – lying out on the mattresses to the sound of the guitar – those first times that Smithy and I drove from Purley down to the coast.

I look down at Smithy and realise that he's managed to get the table together. He pulls himself up from his knees and gives a small bow, nearly toppling over as he waves his hands with a grandiose flourish. That gesture is Smithy as he used to be. There was always something of the magician in him. Together we cut up Joyce's solid vanilla sponge and have two slices each. Then I dig in my pockets and find the cigarettes and matches. I light one for Smithy and put my chair close to his so I can be sure he won't burn himself.

Always good to see the sea, Smithy says.

Yes, I say. I always like a day in Eastbourne.

Smithy looks at me, nods his head, raises one tufty eyebrow and, looking into those cloudy eyes, I have the sense that he knows it all. We pack up the tea things. The sun has gone in and we've had the best of the day. I watch Smithy haul himself up into the van and I take his handkerchief from him and put it in his top pocket, folding it neatly. He stares down at it, pleased by that. I get in the van and we set off.

I drive slowly now, measuring the miles. How many more days out? How many more? I miss Smithy. I miss him so much. He has always been my best friend. And as we slide down towards it – so slowly, so very slowly – it's Smithy who'll have the last laugh, as he always has done. Smithy will go quiet and happy and I'll be raging, raging, and my God, please, please, I only hope he's there to keep me company on that last journey. Not to Eastbourne, or Rye, not from Purley down to the coast, no not there.

# Maria Grech Ganado

## Rhythm

Between this blanket of soil
and the wheeling bed-rock –
sometime, we must have met;
your hand like a knot of roots
must have found my kernel of breast,
and your mouth, a bubble of air,
sucked its tightness –

till there were shoots, and leaves
and petals that came and came
in prisms like waves, leaping up
beyond skies away from the earth.
Under the soil we must
have generated planets.

Today, your hand lies gnarled
and withered on the laundered sheet
of a human room.  My nipples are shrunk
and hard like nuts, my body a parchment
nobody writes new poems on.  But
Nature's rhythms cannot be
just rotting succulence, wasted rain.

This is the human season of drawn curtains,
of windows shut on disinfected rooms,
of tiptoeing to bedheads, of silence,
withheld breath, of trying to pretend
we will not stir in the darkness
between blanket and bed yet again.

# Mary Robinson:

## *House and universe*

*On a time lapse satellite photograph of the world at night*

The beads of light are threaded round the world
like fairy lights in tawdry bars.
I scan the picture for blanks –
blue is mountains deserts forests
black is inland lakes,
the sea marbles the page with gritty school ink.

I flick a switch and imagine a world turning,
points of light joining up
like a child's dot to dot drawing.
My house is there somewhere
blurred in with the rest –
camp-fires street-lamps houses factories fireworks
explosions arson bombings.

Lapsed time lithograph –
some lights are already extinguished
new ones are alight.
This photograph is a lie:
it is night all over the world
the earth snared in apocalyptic darkness
nothing will grow in this artificial glow.

All day my house has turned towards the sun
the pores of its stones soaking in heat
the skin of its paint bleaching and bubbling.
I make a last tour of the garden at dusk,
nebulae of elder flowers and wild rose in the hedge
the safe childhood smell of honeysuckle
fledged housemartins swooping in ever widening orbits
from their mud splodge under the eaves.
Above the horizon a satellite
catches the light of the setting sun
and throws it back to me.

# November

November. No frost.
Summer's seeds
are growing
out of season.

At eleven
I dig parsnips'
white bones
from the earth.

In a pavement crack
a poppy flowers.
Bible paper petals
wisp in the wind.

Swans skid down
on the firth
where once Catalinas
moored for Atlantic patrol.

# Crane

*The crane, that has totally forsaken this country, bred familiarly in our marshes.*
Thomas Pennant Zoology 1768

Water silts into one grazing level, fields breathe
the sweet smell of cattle inked against a sky's torn edge.

A rare vagrant hieroglyph, vertical in a flat land,
picks gobbets out of this water meadow soup.

In every language it is gutteral - grus grus, garan, crane,
gru, geranion. But this one has a mandala's silence:

feathers ash grey as burnt paper, red eyes to scan me,
the dowdy bustle of a dancer with no partner.

It struggles to take off, dragging chains of myth –
constellation, satellite, heavenly messenger,

harbinger of spring; a young girl folding paper cranes –
strange pilgrimage for her feather tipped fingers.

# The Shoe
## Pat Hillyer

'Stop'

Raymond slammed his foot on the brake pedal and just as quickly snatched it off again. The car juddered in protest and beads of sweat broke out on his forehead.

'Why didn't you stop?'

Why should he stop? 'It doesn't matter.' Raymond wiped the sweat running down into his eyes with the back of his hand.

'A shoe left lying in the road does matter. Go back and pick it up.'

'It's only a shoe. I'm not going back.' His snort was dismissive. He might go back for a pair, but just for one was ridiculous. His burst of jerky laughter lacked humour. He jabbed his foot on the accelerator, drawing in his breath sharply as the sudden, clumsy movement caused the car to swerve.

'You're going too fast.'

Of course he was going too fast. He wanted to get away from the damned shoe. Increasing his foot pressure, he hurtled into a vortex of swirling fields, trees and hedges; a landscape rushing towards and engulfing him, but not his thoughts; not blotting those out. They clung on, sweaty and tenacious.

'It'll be reported.'

'A shoe won't be reported.'

'Oh, yes it will. It was a woman's shoe.'

It was still only a shoe and he was not going back for a shoe. He put his foot down. The car responded, surging forward until he had to brake hard for the car in front. On a long sweeping bend it was impossible to see ahead to overtake.

'Slow down, you silly fool. You're going to have an accident.'

Raymond dropped his speed, watching the needle fall back to dither on forty. He was not a silly fool but he would be, if he reported a shoe.

'Good Afternoon, sergeant. There's a shoe lying in the middle of the road and it's going to get run over.'

He shook his head, trying to clear all impressions, of the shoe from his thoughts. The police would not be interested.

'They'll be interested in a woman's shoe.'

Randy cops. 'A shoe is a shoe. They don't have sex.'

Raymond grinned, an owlish grin, remembering the smutty jokes behind desktop lids. What does a navy sling-back and a loafer make? A slipper. What does a pen and an inkwell make? A blot. But his sniggering couldn't blot out the anxiety of his thoughts.

'A woman's shoe is different, it's a give away.'

'Of course women's shoes are different, but they certainly aren't give-aways.'

They were usually damned expensive, and uncomfortable. 'Oh, my poor feet!' With a bunion the size of a duck egg.

'It could have been kicked off by a walker.'

'Just one shoe?'

'It could have fallen out of a rambler's nap-sack.'

'It's the wrong sort of shoe, and in any case walkers walk down the middle of fields, not the middle of roads.'

'Okay!' He was giving in, as always. 'It must have dropped off.'

'Of course it dropped off. It wouldn't be lying in the road if it hadn't dropped off. You useless, smelly old fool.'

Raymond's lower lip trembled. Fifty wasn't that old. He tried to sniff under his armpits and nearly lost control of the car. For a hair-raising moment, he was wobbling across the other side of the double white-line. The sharp intake of breath seemed to fill the car, whether there was any undesirable body odour was immaterial, he was too busy getting the car back on an even-keel to be concerned about stinky armpits and over-active sweat glands. The facial ones were very over-active; he glanced quickly in the rear-view mirror. His sparse ginger hair was glued to a wet forehead.

'You're disgusting.'

He was disgusting. And from now on he was going to enjoy being disgusting. He increased his foot-pressure on the accelerator again.

'You do realise, don't you, that a woman's shoe lying in the

115

road could mean a woman's been murdered.'

Raymond's knuckles whitened, he poked his head forward. Being short of stature, his chin was almost resting on the steering wheel. He was trying to recall the moment he had seen the shoe, lying on the road as if someone, a woman of course, had just stepped out of it – no leg, just the shoe. The half-panic as he had lifted his foot off the accelerator and drifted over it, expecting a clonk as it hit the underside of the car. He had looked back through the rear-view mirror, seeing it still there, untouched, in the middle of the road. It was some minutes before the thought formed in his mind – that he should go back and pick it up. Minutes that covered a mile, and then another mile and after that, the miles were compulsive.

Why should a woman's shoe lying in the road mean there had been a murder? A man's shoe wouldn't cause such speculation. It was sex discrimination. A man's body could be left to rot. He shuddered at the thought of worms borrowing into flesh, his flesh. Any flesh. Pink, young, money-grubbing flesh. Just the possibility of a woman's body and it was police sirens, fire engines and the works. He wasn't going to get involved.

'It's anything for a quiet life with you, isn't it? Anyone can walk over you.'

'With one shoe on.'

Raymond's laughter was wild, manic, over-long; bordering on hysteria. He knew it was, but couldn't stop. Didn't want to stop. Didn't want to stop and go back for a shoe left lying in the road.

'Exactly.'

He repeated the word. 'Exactly.' It was a horrible word; he hated it. He chewed at the inside of his cheek. Exactly should be struck from the dictionary. But words weren't really horrible. It was the way they were said and repeated that was horrible.

'You've got to go back. The shoe fell off when the murderer dragged the body into the copse; that's obvious.'

Was it that obvious? It was only a shoe in the road for heaven's sake. He riddled in the seat; he was so tense his seat-bones were cramping, his bottom going numb. He needed a cushion. A water-cushion, wobble, wobble, slop.

'How about a waterbed?' That shut her up, there was no

answer.

Raymond fantasised over a four-poster with a water mattress. It made him feel buoyed up, floating on water, bonking on water. He bounced on the car-seat, it improved the circulation. He swung the car out to overtake a lorry and only just got back in time. An ear-splitting horn-blast drifted away on the wind. It unnerved him. Undid the buoyancy.

'That was stupid. But you are stupid. A stupid little man.'

Raymond bit his lip; he was not stupid. He'd seen the car coming towards him and he had plenty of time. Well, enough time. That's all one wanted, enough time. The other driver had increased his speed on purpose to frighten him.

'You blame everyone else for your own stupidity. At least stop being so stupid over the shoe, and go back for it.'

Raymond sucked in his lips, his knuckles threatening to burst through the freckly skin as he gripped the steering wheel. He was not going back; he was digging his heels in.

'You're digging your own grave. You can rot in it, eaten by worms. Although you would probably make them sick, just as you make me sick.'

He felt the sneer. He shook himself, trying to shake off the sneer. He was an ordinary man, wanting an ordinary life. He blinked away tears. Love and respect, was that too much to ask of a relationship? He thought of the adverts in the 'lonely hearts' columns. He always scanned them, read them, even noting the call numbers. Torn up into tiny bits and quickly binned. TLC – GSOH – N/S, but it was the 'Maybe more' that he liked.

'I want a partner.'

'In crime?'

'In life.'

'Until death do us part.'

Raymond nodded. He nodded to the sound of the car engine until his head ached and the wheels on a freshly re-surfaced section went – go back, go back, go back, until he rammed his foot down on the accelerator.

'You'll kill us both. Stop the car now and go back for the shoe.'

Now that really was funny. Raymond quickly glanced down at

his watch. It was too late anyway to go back. 'My dinner will be on the table.'

'It's Sunday.'

Oh, Yes! It was Sunday, not Monday or Tuesday, but Sunday.

'You'd better tell the police.'

'That it's Sunday?' Raymond's laughter echoed round the car like the forced, short-burst laughter that accompanied comedy-shows, irritatingly drowning out the next funny bit. And the funny bit was – the police would not be interested in the day of the week.

'But they would be interested in a woman's shoe lying in the road.'

'A shoe lying in the road leads the cops to a corpse in the copse.' Raymond sang the words, tapping the steering wheel with his fingers and the pedals with his foot. 'A shoe lying in the road leads the cops to a corpse in the copse'. The car swerved violently as he struggled to get his handkerchief out to wipe the spittle from the corners of his mouth.

'You're being silly. But then you are silly. A silly little man.'

It was turning into a lovely evening after a cloudy, chilly day; as so often happens in early summer. The sun, low in the sky, bursting into a golden glow as it settled down in a pink-orange duvet cloud, shot with fiery-red streaks.

The bright evening light flickering through the branches of the overhanging trees made Raymond blink and he pulled down the sun-visor. He had never been allowed to appreciate things. He nestled his buttocks comfortably into the seat and opened the neck of his shirt, resting his arm along the window-ledge.

'That's a dangerous thing to do.'

But he wasn't listening. Easing his foot right up, he was cruising along, enjoying his surroundings, familiar and yet not familiar. For the first time he was taking in the loveliness of the country road, the dappling of leaf-pattern on the surface and the peace and quiet disturbed only by the hum of the car engine: a companionable sound. He started humming to it.

'You'll never get far enough away.'

The happy smile crumpled on Raymond's face. Damn the shoe. It was spoiling the evening. It was going to spoil everything.

The car in front stopped suddenly, indicating a right-turn into The Majestic: very majestic with a crenellated entrance. Of course, that was it: the hotel was holding a 'Murder Weekend' with clues littering the road. Raymond upped a finger, after the car had turned in, and grinned. The shoe was a clue. It had nothing to do with him.

The flood of relief was hesitant. It had to be encouraged, nurtured. Raymond worked on it, humming *All things bright and beautiful* off key, his head lolling from side to side on the headrest. Sunday was a day of rest, a day of prayer. *All things bright and beautiful* changed to *Onward Christen Soldiers, marching as to war.*

He heard the laugh. It wasn't a nice laugh.

'With your flat-feet and pigeon-chest you were never near the front-line. You weren't a proper soldier.'

He'd wanted to be a proper soldier. But that was all a long time ago, and he had only served two years.

'In the Pay-Corps!'

Happy moments were always spoilt. He couldn't remember when any of his 'happy moments' had managed to get beyond a split-second. The warmth of a moment just nudging towards existence, and being stamped on – by a shoe.

A shoe! Raymond felt the stamping and crushing of dreams. He sank down into the seat, hiding; wanting to be blotted out. His face was hot and puffy, his breathing heavy. He was crawling along: a man rebuked.

He tried to get back to his appreciation of the evening, but his head was full of aching thoughts. The mask of a grin formed on his face, glued to it, and for the first time he turned his head and looked towards the passenger seat.

'Keep your eyes on the road.'

Even with them on the road, the emptiness of the seat drew his eyes back with furtive sidelong glances. He was only half concentrating on the twists and bends of the road as that emptiness filled him. Turned him to ice. An unexpected loneliness gripped him; the beauty of the evening forgotten and sinking into twilight; leaving him shivering in the cold car.

He struggled to latch onto any noise. But every sound, every vibration, was muted and drifting away from him. He leaned over and poked the radio button. Evensong: shrill, going through his head, he hit the radio with a fist. Tears ran down his face as he nursed bruised knuckles between his knees. The car slowed, fading as it met a hill under-powered, Raymond's foot hardly putting any pressure on the accelerator. He was crumpling, folding-in on himself.

On a bend, the engine cut out and the car sat down like a slaughtered animal. Raymond dropped his head on the steering wheel, hard, wanting hurt. Lifting his head, bang, bang, wanting to batter his skull: so full of unquiet thoughts. He sobbed as he nursed the bruising. After all, he had to go back.

Hot tears mingled with hotter sweat, running down his face, almost blinding him as he botched a three-point turn amidst a sudden flurry of road activity. Rush hour for Evening Service. Church bells ringing. 'Christ!' Shunting back and forth, meeting verge and hitting wall. Prolonged tooting. 'Christ!' And some of the language issuing from angrily rolled down windows was not fit for the Sabbath.

Raymond shunted and another stone dropped out of the wall; his tyre ground over it as the car bumped up on the opposite verge and bounced along in the ruts.

Through the windscreen, Raymond's face was putty white, sunken eyed, like a death's head. He had left his tin of handmade trout-flies perched on the tree stump down by the lake. He had forgotten them. Hours of laborious, but loving work had gone into their making. The fine fiddling with his hands could somehow shut out his immediate surroundings. He made lots of flies. But It wasn't their value, sentimental or otherwise, it was the fact that they had been so carelessly left on the tree stump.

'You're not going back for the shoe then.'

'Fuck the shoe. The flies will be found.'

'So will the shoe.'

'To Hell with the bloody shoe!'

'Swearing shows lack of control.'

He had never been more in control. Sitting straight-backed with his hands at ten-to-two, eyes glued to the road. There was a desperate purpose now in going back.

In the fast fading light, as Raymond got within the vicinity of

120

the fishing lake, he kept his eyes focused above the surface of the road. He was determined not to see the shoe. He was going back for his tin of flies, not for the shoe. He had no intention of stopping to pick up the shoe.

'You may as well pick it up.'

He was not picking it up. Anyway it was getting too dark to see it.

As he approached the copse, with the road narrowing and in heavy shadow from high hedges, he did feel a slight bump and wondered if he'd run over the shoe. It was going to get run over. He pictured the flattened leather, the heel broken off and crushed. A small night-time animal squashed in the road, unrecognisable.

Raymond parked in the small lay-by by the Forestry Commission opening; the log was already across and padlocked. He ducked under and wandered down the rough track. It was creepy and chill in the shadows under the trees as he approached the lake. Cold fingers ran up and down his spine in time to the creak and groan of the branches in a stirring evening breeze. Whispered secrets. There was one more to tell now. Putting his hands over his ears, he slithered down the bank to the water's edge, feeling a flood of relief as he made out his tin of flies still on the stump where he had left it.

He picked up the tin, the last rays of sunlight danced on the water, glistening ripples winking at him, murmuring to him – we won't tell, we won't tell – he shuddered and looked over at the clubhouse at the far end, wondering how the match had gone, who'd won. He never fished in a match. Annette was always with him.

He thought of Annette. During the week, he went into the city by train. He usually caught the 5.05 back, which meant he was home by six o'clock. Precisely at six, Annette put his dinner on the table. Some nights though, he had to work late, or the train was late, or even cancelled – that had happened more than once – but his dinner was always on the table at six o'clock. She was like that.

All week, he waited for Sunday. They didn't have dinner on a Sunday. They had a snack he prepared when they got back from the fishery. Standing on the bank, wading into the shallows, he could lose himself in the water. He could imagine himself in a different world: a watery, peaceful world. Casting, watching, waiting – flick, flick, flick, he could shut everything else out.

Annette's voice had a piercing quality. She disturbed the fish. She disturbed the others and they said she disturbed the fish. It was embarrassing. But he could usually shut that out too.

Today had been the match. They didn't want him in the team. He understood.

It was deep and weedy where he was standing. There were no fish at the tree-end.

The teams would be in the Hand & Garter discussing the day's sport. Drinking to the winners. Looking over the water, he fancied he could hear them. The laughter, the banter, the clinking of glasses – 'It's your round.' 'No it's not.' 'It is.' 'I bought the last lot in.' 'Well you got the biggest fish.' 'It was a whopper, wasn't it.' 'It wouldn't have fitted in the glass.' 'It wouldn't have liked the beer' – They were a decent crowd. Not that he really knew any of them, always having to stay on the periphery, never able to join in.

Raymond's head jerked up, listening intently, his musings frozen. Leaf-mulch and twigs scrunched and crackled, someone was approaching. He tried to sink back into the shadows, crouching like a cornered animal.

'Here boy! Here!'

Raymond let out a shriek as something landed in the reed-bed right beside him, flopping and shooting muddy water straight into his face.

'Jock! Come here boy.'

Jock leapt back onto the bank, shaking vigorously, giving Raymond a shower as he tried to stand up, his feet slipping and sliding in the mud.

'Sorry mate. Hey! Is that you Ray? What' you doing here?'

Raymond stood shivering from shock, icy water running down his face. He didn't look at Brian. He looked down at his splashed trousers, and with a shaking hand started wiping at them.

'Sorry Ray. Sit! Sit! You bad dog. You weren't fishing in the match were you?' Brian took a step forward, peering through the gloom. 'I didn't see you.'

'No.'

'Thought not. Here, let me give you a hand.' Brian leaned forward grabbing lumps of him as Raymond struggled for a foothold on the slippery bank.

Making sure Raymond was unlikely to slide back amongst the reeds, Brian looked nervously around, his eyes searching the shadows. 'Where's Annette?'

Raymond shook his head.

Brian's gaze again poked at the trees. 'Is she in the car?'

'She didn't come.'

'Oh!' Brian nodded, not fully convinced, his eyes still drifting. 'Then why didn't you join us?'

'It was late.'

'Wouldn't have mattered. You should have come over, the lads would have understood. You missed a good match.' His wavering look went over Raymond's shoulder. 'We missed you.'

Like hell you did. Giving a twisted grin, Raymond turned away. He wanted to end the conversation. He wanted Brian to go.

But Brain appeared to be settling, a little uncertain still, but not planning any immediate departure. 'Bill's team won. Six beauts and not one under three pounds. You should have come over.'

'I said I was late.' He hadn't meant to snap. He was doing his best to keep cool.

'Okay mate. Keep your hair on.'

'Sorry.'

'Not to worry.' Brian tried to reach out with an arm-pat, but missed as Raymond stepped away from him and he settled for a chummy nod instead, to show he understood. Raymond's Annette was a standing joke at the club. They made fun behind his back, but it was harmless. They liked Ray and felt sorry for him. Brian's eyes nervously searched the shadows, as if his thoughts might cause an unwanted manifestation. Feeling reassured, he suggested, 'You had a row?' And again he moved forward into touch, just in case a little matey sympathy was required.

Raymond didn't answer immediately. Only heavy breathing and dog panting disturbed the evening.

Shrugging, Brian broke the silence. 'Well you should come on your own.' Again his eyes raked the shadows suspiciously, still half-expecting Annette to suddenly appear. She was so much a part of Raymond's fishing tackle. He quietly observed the tin of flies clutched in Raymond's hand.

Raymond, having given up trying to get away, stood with his shoulders hunched, perhaps Brian would go if he explained. 'It was late because I took Annette to the station. She's gone to be with her sister.'

'Ah!' Brian nodded. Darkness was falling quickly, the moon, not yet come into its own. It was going to be difficult to see their way back. 'In that case you should have come over. No one would have minded you being late. You shouldn't have stayed on your own. I know the feeling mate.' Brian sniffed and looked out over the water. 'You catch nowt here. Not under the trees. Too dark. And too weedy.'

His whistle went right through Raymond's head. 'Come on boy.' The spaniel bounded up and Brian turned away, waving, calling out 'see you' as he crashed back into the trees the way he had come.

Raymond stood listening to dog and master going away, and as the noise of their passage lessened, still stood, locked to the spot, feeling sick and going over and over what he'd said. Not much; but an inner voice was warning him that it was still too much.

It had been the silence. The silence had got inside him. All the way to the fishery Annette had gone on and on, insisting that he should fish in the match. How could he, with her there? She was the reason Bill had not asked him to fish, and his team had won. As always, he'd missed out. He couldn't fish in the match, but he wasn't going to miss his Sunday fishing. He'd driven in through the forestry track to fish on his own at the far end, under the trees – losing half his tackle in the weeds.

Annette wouldn't get out of the car. He'd been grateful at first. But she sat there all day, not saying a word.

Her silence had bored into his back, until he couldn't breathe. His line kept getting caught up and her silence was digging into him; turning his insides to raw fish-guts. By mid-afternoon, he couldn't stand it any longer and he'd gone over to make her talk. He'd leant into the car to squeeze out the words. All those belittling, nagging words that he knew were there. He couldn't shut them out if they weren't said.

Raymond moved; his whole body stiff, awkward, tripping over tree roots, lurching against tree trunks; not really picking his way, stumbling; grunting, beyond cursing. Damn Brian, poking his nose in.

Reaching the lay-by, he staggered, as if inebriated, along the road until he reached the shoe. It was still there. Not run over. He picked it up, stroking the soft kid-leather, pressing it against his cheek. It smelt of shoe, of her. Carrying it to the car, he placed it on the seat beside him and drove slowly down the road.

It had been foolhardy stopping the car and dragging her across the lane in broad daylight; heaving her over the stile – imagining that if anyone saw him he would look as though he was helping her over – flopping like a rag-doll! The gorse and bramble tore at him and tripped him up. He'd not gone far in, just to the first clump of bushes. He'd parked in a passing place and could have caused a mini traffic-jam of onlookers, but he was lucky. Late Sunday afternoon, there was not another living soul in sight. Driving off, he'd seen the shoe.

He was covering his tracks. But it was too late. Brian had seen him. Panic was gripping him, hands shaking, trying to hum, picking up the sound of the engine; even opening a window to hear the sound of his tyres on the road as he went over dried mud and stones from a tractor. For over a mile there had been no other car and the wind was cold, freezing – his right ear was numb and his head ached.

A kid-leather sling-back was not really the sort of shoe to wear under the trees down by the lake. It was entirely the wrong sort of shoe. He didn't really want it in the car. He reached over and picked it up, meaning to fling it out of the window, but it was awkward and it dropped down inside the car between his seat and the door. Going round a bend, the shoe became involved with his feet. For moments he played footsie, then reached down, feeling for it. Sobbing, he got hold of the shoe and put it back on the seat.

Annette and her sister Margaret were both dead now.

They'd been visiting Margaret when she died, falling down stairs and breaking her neck. He preferred Margaret; he'd married the wrong sister. He'd tried to kiss her. She pushed him away and

125

slipped. Annette was arguing with a delivery-boy; totally out of place in someone else's home, but Annette was like that. Margaret was the quiet one. Dear, sweet Margaret.

He heard the laugh. It went right through his body.

Escape! He slammed his foot down on the accelerator and the car surged forward, faster, faster; he was overtaking without looking, without caring; headlights, blaring horns. A car coming towards him flashed, full-beam, he couldn't see a damn thing. Damn fool! The near-side front tyre caught the verge, a glancing slither, but for desperate moments the car span out of control, leaving him sitting in a pool of sweat.

Taking the next turning left, he pulled up, closed his eyes – sinking into the seat. Brian would tell. He felt in the glove compartment, something soft, and wiped his face. Annette's smell shot up his nose, Chanel something and damned expensive like the shoes. He dropped the glove.

He shouldn't have gone back at all. Dropping the shoe had been unfortunate. Leaving the tin of flies, forgetful. It could be days before Annette's body was found. Some dog-walker, they were usually the ones to find bodies. The tin of flies may never have been found. Who in their right mind fishes at the tree end? He should not have gone back.

Tears rolled down Raymond's face. He had longed, ached, for Annette to shut up. And when she did, he couldn't stand it. The silence was worse. Margaret's death had been her own fault, pushing him away like that in disgust. Annette's death had been her own fault too.

He could dispose of the shoe. But Brian knew he'd been there. Brian would tell.

Raymond raised his head, squinting through the windscreen. A full moon, a fool's moon. The road looked hard and white as if in cold, clear daylight. He knew the road; in half a mile it curved off to the right, leading to the clubhouse side of the lake, the main entrance and car park.

It was a pity about Brian. He'd only got his dog. His wife had died of cancer over a year ago; a nice little woman who used to do tea and sandwiches for the clubhouse, now Brian did it on his own.

126

He and Annette usually left early. They didn't socialise. Annette thought them a rough lot and what they thought of Annette had long since ceased to be of concern. By mid afternoon, he was usually glad to pack up and head for home. It was easier that way.

Brian could easily have walked his dog the other way. It was conspiracy. Annette had lured Brian there, just as she had encouraged him to go back for the shoe.

Raymond turned into the empty car park and pulled up. He wandered round the timber structure with its corrugated roof, peering in through the windows, tasting the thrill of sneak-thief; the trespass of memories. He could feel the after-throb of the day's sport all around him. The noisy, backslapping departures. Cars starting up, churning and crunching the gravel. 'See you next Sunday.' And the final emptiness. The settling of silence.

Raymond knew all about silence. He knew it wasn't silent, it was an echo that one couldn't get at. It was a penetrating sound just out of reach, the decibels piercing one's head, cooking one's brain. Words spoken out aloud could be heard, and ignored. Silence could not be ignored and in the end, it got at you. Silence was all around him now in the deserted car park.

Raymond threw the shoe. Tossing it far into the lake; watching until the glistening black surface was again flat and undisturbed in the stillness of the night. He climbed back into his car and turned right out of the car park, Brian's cottage was only half a mile down the lane.

# Paul Jeffcutt

## Homestead

Down the end of the abandoned lane,
between stubby fields
of nettles, couch-grass and docks,
the old house squatted.
A muddied cattle-trail led to the empty gate
and wandered on;

choked to the lintels with briars,
rotten window-frames gaped –
beyond drooping slates, a sycamore
where rooks refused to nest.
Forcing thorns apart, he stepped in:
it was putrid, quiet,

above the barren grate, a tiled mantelpiece
shrouded with cobwebs and the drained bodies of insects
that kicked their last as Jim Reeves crooned on the radio –
filthy strands held a deserted toy soldier,
in the mildew beside him
a teddy bear's eye.

Shattered tiles crunched to the thick, square sink,
(where stains couldn't be erased)
and a careworn, enamel cooker,
its oven door clasped by bramble spines –
still guarding against the ungrateful child
who wanted.

# Tides

I wanted to stay 1ater, last night:
my smiles furrowed the drapes,
eddying around the thickets
of your cheese planted, rocking-chair parlour.
Luminously, Van played and you stroked,
stretched tabby, silky tailed,
purring the talking hours of our biosphere.

But I began to lose my bearings,
like that strange summer
                    of escape
to the verdant island;
roaming the broody mountains,
switchbacks edging through the pines –
        drenched and astray.

Katrina Naomi

## The Sculptor's Studio

This room: tins of Peak Freens proffer scourers
and wooden-handled mallets; an old jar
of Maxwell House; and brazenly fluted
bottles of Johnny Walker's, with a rag
for a stopper, filled with red and yellow
ground nut oil, reminding me of Brixton
market. Here, the oils have set for decades.
They no longer smoothe Ms Hepworth's wood,
but these West African oils watch over
their adopted Cornish sculptures-to-be.
Already they have form — but are stillborn.
Step outside, step into her garden. Look:

the sarcophagus-cum-birdbath, passage
to the gods. Can you see her, sewing stone?

# The Years of Coal

Here are the rooms that I've put together
with a corridor and stairs,
where the spider lived.
That house is the scene
of all short stories, novels and radio plays.

That room with the bunkbeds
and the green and black condensation,
like no chocolate,
where 1 asked him
if he'd be our new father.

That kitchen, when we arrived,
a bitter pattern, the careful scorch of an iron,
on every tile, a fresh frieze around the wall.
And my mother's tears --
though I'm told I don't remember these.

The flat roof of the coal shed,
where I'd listen to the Top 40,
every Sunday. Writing each song down,
watching form like a bookie, in a bikini,
with a transistor, and a view of the flats.

The pink and blue hydrangea,
the lily of the valley,
on either side of the redbrick steps --
the welcoming to all that would happen in that house.
Some of which might still be too enormous to tell.

# Birdsongs are Composed of Love Notes and Pleasure Notes

There is no dictionary, so I sit with a tape recorder and notebook, pressing buttons, listening and writing. I've learnt basic Pheasant. Blackbird and Robin I'm struggling with.

1 don't have the right shaped beak and my throat is too large. There is a robin who sits by me. I can't understand if it's love, and I'm worried. How would we kiss?

I imagine he'd be good with his wings. I can feel the rub of his little chest. But I can't give him any more, not yet, just the slightest of caresses. I haven't the words.

# Contributors:

**Denise Bennett** has an MA in creative writing and teaches adult education classes in this subject. Her work has been widely published in magazines and in anthologies used for worship; her work is broadly spiritual. In 2004 she won the Hamish Canham prize for the best poem published in Poetry Society newsletter.

**Helen Cadbury** has had poems published by Staple Magasine, by the Cinnamon Press and in the Arvon International Poetry Competition anthology. Her short story, Nature's Way, was produced as a Radio 4 afternoon story in February 2008. Helen is currently writing a novel and working on a literacy project in a women's prison.

**Catherine Chanter** grew up in the West Country and studied English at St. Anne's College, Oxford. After several years as a lobbyist in the UK and abroad, she re-trained as a teacher, specialising in supporting children with behavioural difficulties. She currently works at The Tavistock in London. Apart from short stories and poetry, Catherine has also written for Radio 4.

**Maureen Gallagher** lives and works in Galway. She's had poetry and prose published in literary magazines worldwide and broadcast on RTE. She's been shortlisted for awards many times, including The Flat Lake Poetry award 2007, Poetry Now 2006 Award. Maureen's website can be viewed at www.maureengallagher.net

**Maria Grech Ganado** (b. 1943), studied at the Universities of Malta, Cambridge and Heidelberg. She has published three collections of Maltese poetry (winning the National Book Prize in 2002) and two of English. In 2000, Maria received *Il-Qadi tar-Repubblika* medal for Service to the Republic as the first Maltese woman to be appointed full-time lecturer at the University of Malta. Her poetry in both languages has been translated into nine others. Maria has three children.

**Jean Harrison** is retired, writing steadily and has poetry published in a number of magazines. Her poem 'Woman on the Moon' was short-listed for the Forward Prize in 2004. Her first collection is forthcoming with Cinnamon Press.

**Pat Hillyer** writes – Not a bad year for short stories: third prize in Penguin Book sponsored competition and three highly commended in University of Winchester Writers' Festival, plus one on the Internet: Arvon Arts Foundation making me a Laureate Friend for the year. And of course 'The Shoe' which I hope you will enjoy. Unfortunately, my latest short story is trying to become full length – I have been taken over by a man named George on the run…

**Mavis Howard** used to think she was more of a playwright (and once received a Guinness Award for pub theatre) but now writes mostly poetry, which is published here and there.

**Clare Jay** teaches Dreaming into Creative Writing workshops and Hatha yoga. Her doctoral thesis focused on the connection between lucid dreaming and creative writing, which enabled her to carry out significant parts of her research while asleep. She enjoys swimming in waking life and flying in her dreams.

**Paul Jeffcutt** is a member of the writer's group at the Seamus Heaney Centre for Poetry in Belfast. His poetry has been published in journals and anthologies in Britain, Ireland and Australia. Paul has read his work at numerous venues across Ireland. He lives amidst the drumlins in the peaceful green countryside of South Down.

**Alice Jolly** has published two novels – *What the Eye Doesn't See* and *If Only You Knew* (both published by Simon and Schuster). She teaches creative writing for the Open University and lives in Brussels.

**Marianne Jones** grew up on Ynys Mon/Anglesey in North Wales. Her work has appeared in several literary magazines, (*New Welsh Review, Coffee House Poetry, Borderlines, Envoi, Haiku Quarterly,* etc.) and in anthologies: *An Anglesey Anthology* (Gwasg Carreg Gwalch), *The Lie of the Land* (Cinnamon Press), *Changing Times* and *Even the Rain is Different* (Honno Women's Press). Her first collection of poetry, *Too Blue for Logic,* is to be published by Cinnamon Press in April, 2009.

**Miceál Kearny** was born in 1980. He lives in the West of Ireland and works on the family farm; the eldest in a family of four. He has read in Ireland, England, Slovenia and Chicago. Miceál was winner of the Baffle, Cúirt and Cuisle poetry grand slams and short-listed for the 2007 Cinnamon Press Poetry Award.

**Doreen King** is General Secretary of the British Haiku Society. In 2005, she won the Presence Award for haiku, and was awarded the Suseki Publishing Prize of the Kaji Aso Studio International Haiku Contest. In 2006, she was given the Kyoto Museum for World Peace Award at the 40th A-Bomb Memorial Day Haiku Meeting.

**Catherine Matthews** was born in South Wales and now lives in London. Cry Baby is her first foray into short story writing. She is currently working on a novel, and studying creative writing at City University.

**Ann McManus** - Originally from Northern Ireland, Ann did an English degree at the University of Ulster where she was awarded the 'Walter Allen Prize for Creative Writing'. She has had travel articles published and a short story 'Moths' was published in a quarterly 'Writing Ulster'. She lives in Penarth with her husband and two children.

**Katrina Naomi** is originally from Margate and tries to write every day. She is starting an MA in Creative Writing at Goldsmiths and hopes to still find time for walking long-distance paths with her partner, sherry drinking, dancing, travel, friends, jazz and reading crime novels.

**Mary Robinson** lives in Cumbria where she teaches English literature in higher and adult education. Llŷn, where she has spent much of her life, has been an important influence on her poetry. She was shortlisted for the Templar Poetry Prize in 2007.

**Derek Sellen** writes poetry, short stories and plays. He teaches English language and literature in Canterbury and writes grammar books for EFL students which attempt not to be boring. His poems have appeared in various magazines, newspapers and anthologies and been awarded prizes in national and international competitions.

**Ruth Thompson**, who lives and works in Belfast, began writing poetry around eight years ago and obtained an MA in creative writing at Queen's University. Her poetry influences include Michael Longley, Liz Lochhead and Vona Groarke, and her work is flavoured by archaeology, birds, loughs and islands. She is working on a first collection.

**Deborah Trayhurn** has moved frequently, so losing and finding have been constant themes. Now settled in rural Scotland, landscape and the elements, along with the human predicament, shape poems and paintings. Besides teaching, is working on a collection, emboldened by appearances in anthologies, winning or being placed in competitions.

**Rhys Trimble** is a bilingual poet working in north Wales. He was born in Livingstone Zambia, and brought up in Pontneddfechan in south Wales. Rhys has published poetry in *Poetry Wales, Tears in the Fence, Seventh Quarry, Coffee House Poetry* and other magazines. Recent work includes a self-published a chapbook: *afanc e.p.*

**Jan Villarrubia** is a native of New Orleans and an award-winning poet and playwright. She co-founded DramaRama, an annual theatre and performing arts festival in New Orleans; and teaches creative writing. She lost her home the day after Hurricane Katrina when the federal levees broke and is currently rebuilding on her property in a bird sanctuary near the lake. Her collection, *Return to Bayou Lacombe*, will be published by Cinnamon in November 2008.

**Mark Wagstaff** lives and works in London. His new novel, *The Canal*, will be published by Mighty Erudite in 2008. Details at www.mighty-erudite.com He has had a number of short stories published over the last eight years, including recently in *Open Wide, Libbon* and *Texts' Bones*. Mark has self-published two well-received novels, *After Work* and *Claire*, and a collection of short pieces, *Blue Sunday Stories*. Details at www.markwagstaff.com

**Michele Wardall**

**Shelagh Weeks** lives in Cardiff and has three children. For a long time she juggled five jobs (and did little writing), but now has only one job - teaching Creative Writing at Cardiff University. She has just completed a first novel, To Be a Pilgrim, forthcoming with Cinnamon Press.

**Martin Willitts Jr** recent publications are The Secret Language of the Universe (March Street Press, 2006), Lowering Nets of Light (Pudding House Publications, 2007), News from the Front (www.slowtrains.com, 2007), Alternatives to Surrender (Plain View Press, 2007), and Words & Paper (http://www.threelightsgallery.com/mwj, 2008).

**Paul Yoward** writes – What the Who?: What of where I'm from? Where I'm bound most concerns – when will this Loiner breakfast-mcss be done? Where do words take one? Besides Yeats aspiration, I could cite: Orwell's articles; Dylan's introduction – both, all senses – all between them. Hopefully, between-line writing's, not just in the head, previously published pamphlets or merely here, domiciled: Caerdydd. All the rest is my business.